Being an NHS Chief Executive

By Lisa Rodrigues

D1439433

ISBN-13: 978-1-5272-2104-8

Published by
The Laughton Press
contact@thelaughtonpress.co.uk

cover design Ken McLoone

cover photograph by Joseph Rodrigues Marsh

book design Ann Jaloba Publishing

book editing Jean Gray

DEDICATION

For all who choose a life in service of others.
With love and thanks.

Being an NHS Chief Executive

CHAPTERS

Being an NHS Chief Executive

About the author

Lisa Rodrigues CBE is a writer, coach and mental health campaigner. Her NHS career spanned 41 years, first as a nurse and later in health service management, including 13 years as chief executive at Sussex Partnership NHS Foundation Trust, providing mental health and related services in the South East of England.

In 2013, Lisa announced her plans to retire. She then surprised friends and colleagues by coming out about her own experiences of depression, which was almost immediately followed by her worst ever depressive episode. She returned to work in January 2014 and retired in the summer of the same year.

Lisa now uses her understanding of stigma, including self-stigma, to raise awareness and reduce the negativity that is still associated with mental illness. She chaired a two-year project for the charity Time to Change, reporting in July 2016 on the stigma that still exists within mental health services. She coaches executives as well as new NHS clinicians and leaders and is vice chair of the Mary Seacole Trust. Lisa volunteers with Samaritans and helps to run her local branch.

Lisa has a BA in Psychology and an MA in Public Sector Management. She writes a blog www.lisasaysthis.com and is a contributor to publications such as the *Guardian* and *Health Service Journal*. She speaks at conferences and via the broadcast media. You can find her on Twitter @LisaSaysThis.

Lisa also writes fiction. She hopes you will read her first novel one day.

Being an NHS Chief Executive

Foreword

by Professor Dame Elizabeth Anionwu
DBE FRCN FQNI

It is a huge honour to contribute to Lisa's wonderful book! We first met in the late 1970s at a meeting of the Radical Health Visitors group. A few decades later our paths were to cross again and it enabled us to reconnect in a permanent manner. It was in 2011 when I was retired and Vice-Chairperson of the Mary Seacole Memorial Statue Appeal. The NHS Confederation had kindly provided the charity with a stand at their annual conference in Manchester. Suddenly this enthusiastic woman bounded over and began a conversation with me – it was Lisa! She was an NHS Chief Executive and quickly made up her mind to actively support the Appeal and use her connections to help us make the statue a reality. What an action woman! I was invited to talk at her trust's annual nursing conference about Mary Seacole and badges and books were purchased for staff to further aid the fundraising. Lisa was appointed an Ambassador and following the successful unveiling of the statue became Vice-Chair of the Mary Seacole trust.

There is a searing honesty that runs through the chapters. This is particularly apparent when describing the challenges and rewards of senior management as well as Lisa's personal accounts of depression. The constant struggle to develop high quality mental health services is laid out bare, revealing the inequitable resources in contrast to certain other areas of NHS provision.

I would strongly encourage anybody aspiring to reach the upper echelons of the NHS to read Lisa's book.

Being an NHS Chief Executive

Why I wrote this book

Saturday 21 April 2012

I've been staying in Horsham, West Sussex with my mother for a week after a planned hospital admission (her, not me). I have managed my diary so I can be there to help her in the mornings and not leave her alone too long each day; thank goodness for modern technology and kind friends who pop by to keep her company while I go to essential meetings and continue to run the trust.

She says she is feeling better this morning. My brother arrives in time for coffee and takes over before I set off home.

Back in Brighton, an official-looking envelope awaits me. Apparently, it has been there since Wednesday. I open it with trembling fingers. Her Majesty the Queen wonders whether I would be prepared to accept the honour of becoming a Commander of the British Empire (CBE) for services to the NHS.

My head swims.

Thursday 24 May 2012

My father died 20 years ago today, aged 62. My mother and I stroll slowly around the cemetery in the late afternoon sun. I tell her about the CBE (which after some internal turmoil that I don't mention to her, I have decided to accept). It must stay confidential until it is announced next month on the Queen's Birthday. My mother knows the score; she became an Officer of the British Empire (OBE) the year my father died – 1992, the year of the Barcelona Olympics. The queue at the Palace was alphabetical; Matthew Pinsent and Steve Redgrave towered over two small but powerful women - Queen Elizabeth II and my mother.

I tell her she will be coming to the Palace again, with me. She says how proud my father would have been of me, and I thank her, and tell her that he would have been even prouder of her.

This gets me thinking.

Saturday 16 June 2012

My CBE is announced. Kate Winslet also gets one and Tessa Jowell is made a Dame. My executive team surprise me by dressing up in cardboard crowns and draping the boardroom in Union Jacks. I receive over 500 emails and letters of congratulation, while I am still wondering how the naughtiest girl in the Great Ormond Street October 1973 set has managed to fool everyone and get honoured for services to the NHS. It is for this reason, rather than any sense of republicanism, that I hesitated before accepting. But I've done it now. All I need is an outfit for the Palace.

Friday 25 January 2013

In the end, I wear a green jacket and black fascinator combo. My husband, Steve, has a matching green tie. The family scrubs up well. We stay overnight in Belgravia and return from the Palace for lunch with other members of my family and a few friends who have fun trying on my medal. My weekly message to staff and patients starts with 'I wasn't always CBE material'. It gets hundreds of responses. And I think even harder.

Wednesday 25 September 2013

My planned retirement from Sussex Partnership in the summer of 2014 is announced. I will be 59. I made a hash of it the last time I tried to leave, when our daughter was very ill in 2010, so I feel I owe it to my board, colleagues and our staff to do better this time, giving plenty of notice. Apart from a couple of sarcastic online comments about whether I will change my mind again, people are lovely.

Which is good, because I have something bigger planned for the following week.

Thursday 3 October 2013

My article, *A very personal "Personal Best"* about my experiences of depression off and on since the age of 15, is published in the *Health Service Journal* to coincide with the launch of Britain's Personal Best, a post-Olympic legacy charity. Going public is something I have thought about for a very long time.

I am overwhelmed by encouraging feedback. It is apparently the most read *HSJ* opinion piece that year. I speak at the charity launch. People are visibly moved.

The next day is our Great Ormond Street October 1973 Set 40-year reunion, which I have helped to organise, followed by a weekend in Hampstead visiting old haunts with my closest nursing chums. By Sunday night I am feeling surreal. I seem to have given up on sleep.

So begins a strange month in which I become increasingly edgy and irritable. I can't concentrate. I have recurrent stabbing stomach pains and feel sick a lot of the time; I find myself in the small hours researching whether one can regrow a gall bladder (the original one having been jettisoned in 2011). Other irrational acts include drafting a letter to HM the Queen to return the CBE. I am inexplicably close to tears at inappropriate and worryingly frequent moments.

Friday 8 November 2013

Awake through the previous night going over and over how vile I was during new consultant interviews the previous day. The fact that it has taken more than a year for us to replace doctors at a hospital that is desperately in need of strong clinical leadership, doesn't mean I have the right to be a bad-tempered cow.

Arrive at the office feeling loathsome but also strangely disconnected, like being on automatic pilot only the wrong setting.

Everything feels jarring and wrong. People speak, but I can barely make out what they are saying. I don't even bother to try.

Stomach cramps getting worse. Much time spent in the loo. No idea what I am doing, nor do I care. I look in the mirror and see a ghost. Eventually several people tell me I look so terrible that I need to go home.

Leave around 16.00. It is dark and raining, I think. Drive very slowly as I am struggling to think straight. Seriously consider crashing car into the central reservation on the A27 flyover near Lancing College but cannot face the thought of all the fuss if I don't die. Get home eventually. My lovely office administrator has rung to see if I'm OK. Steve v worried. I start crying. I can't stop.

My world falls apart.

Monday 6 January 2014

Against all the odds, I return to work. People know why I have been away, because I've told my chairman and executive team that I want them to be honest. This should make it easier, but it doesn't. What my psychiatrist (not from my own trust, they cannot treat their boss however much you plead with them) called a moderate to severe depressive episode, I think of by the more old-fashioned term of a breakdown.

I've written more about this in Chapter 12. Most leaders who have them never return to work. But I am determined, for my own sake and everyone else's, not to sneak away with my tail between my legs. I have nothing to feel ashamed of, I tell myself, feeling more ashamed than it is possible to describe.

Thursday 9 January 2014

Our twice-yearly Leadership Conference. I am on a return to work programme, coming in to the office for just a few hours each day in my first week back. My colleagues Sue Morris and Sue Esser should run a masterclass on managing a mentally ill chief executive; they are brilliant. Sue M says that I don't need to come to the conference, but I know it will look very odd if I don't. Somehow, I get myself there and sit quietly at the front between the Sues, a change from my usual attempt to say hello to 200 attendees before the formal start.

Sue M introduces me. You could hear a pin drop. I have no idea what I have said, but it seems to go down OK. Apparently one senior clinician whispers to another 'Say what you like about Lisa, but she's got balls'.

It doesn't feel like it.

Thursday 10 July 2014

The second Leadership Conference of the year. A new tradition, we are at the Amex Stadium. My leaving do is held at the same venue in the afternoon. The sun shines. Colm Donaghy, my successor, and I have broken the golden *Dr Who* rule and been seen together several times during the past week.

The theme of the event is shabby chic, with lots of homemade items. Instead of a leaving speech, I do my own awards ceremony and give out hand-made badges based on our six core values. There are some nice photos.

I give the leftover badges to Colm and wish him well.

Friday 11 July 2014

Open house in what is still my office for one more day, and some extraordinary chats with people who drop by.

Again, I leave at 16.00. My new life begins. All I have to do now is write this bloody book.

The book

I honestly didn't set out to become a Chief Executive of an NHS trust. It was more a case of the job choosing me, and I spent 13 years doing it, seven before we became a foundation trust and six afterwards. This is my story about how and why, and some of the things that occurred along the way. It is the opposite of a management book, more a how-not-to guide. I've written it for a bit of personal catharsis, and for anyone who might be interested. I hope it will help people. But I have to be honest and admit that I don't think it would have helped me all that much. Because the only thing that got me to my current level of knowledge and self-awareness (still very much a work in progress) is having lived through those years, plus the ones that came before.

I won't pretend that I have all the answers for you. Only you do. If you have an over-developed sense of responsibility and a burning desire to make things happen, I wish you loving kindness in your chosen career, and the very best of luck along the way. You are going to need both.

Chapter 1

A bit of personal history

I was the oldest of three, one of those annoying children who was always asking questions and wanting to know what was going on. I think I wanted to understand what motivated people, how they related to each other, and how the world was organised. I am still the same. It took me a long time to realise that not everyone is like this. Some people call it being nosey.

I was born in a less than lovely part of West London. We moved to the beautiful county of West Sussex just before my fifth birthday. At my funny little school in Horsham, I often got told off for talking too much. My brother and I stood out because we had an unusual surname; Sussex was not very cosmopolitan in those days.

My first school

St Christopher's was a small private school set in a Victorian house and gardens that had seen better days. None of the teachers were qualified, and there were some unusual teaching methods. The headmistress's study-bedroom was next door to one of our classrooms on the first floor. We were taken there only if we had been very naughty. She was rather glamorous and a theatre lover; school productions were more important than lessons. One Christmas, I was cast as Mary in the nativity play, until one of the teachers said 'oh no, not the little Jewish girl' and a girl with blond plaits called Libby was chosen instead. I only appreciated the irony years later; I wasn't actually Jewish, although my father was. More importantly, so was Mary.

Being an NHS Chief Executive

When I was nine, we relocated to Toronto, Canada because of my father's job. In 1964, the Canadian culture was more open than in England; children were encouraged to ask questions and to find things out for themselves. We had well-qualified, enthusiastic teachers, and we were always writing stories, listening to radio plays, doing projects that involved interviewing people in our local community and carrying out our own research in the school library. I felt more at home amongst the diverse group of children in my Canadian school than back in Horsham. Because I was quite bright and we started school a year earlier in the UK, I was in a class with pupils two or three years older than me; some were teenagers by the time we came back to England in 1966. But I never felt left out, and I missed them and everything about Toronto. In some ways, I always will.

I also loved reading. I read anywhere, walking slowly home from the public library, on the toilet, or with a torch under the bedclothes after I was meant to be asleep. I would bribe my brother so he would let me use his library ticket as well as my own. And I would read anything I could lay my hands on, from Enid Blyton and Louisa May Alcott to Dickens and the Reader's Digest. My father was a prolific reader and owned many books. He was sympathetic to my voracious reading habits.

I loved writing too. I was always writing stories, and my parents predicted that I would become a writer. But as I grew older, I was increasingly drawn to looking after animals and children. Like most big sisters, I took my responsibility for my younger siblings seriously. I loved ponies and dogs but especially cats. My first job, aged 12, was working in a cattery in the summer holidays. Miss Clark, the owner, paid my bus fare plus 10 shillings a week, which I spent on sweets to eat on the bus. Without my help she could whizz round her 40 feline residents in under an hour. It took me all morning to clean out the cages, replenish the litter trays and feed the feline occupants, because I had to take each one out, play with it and give it a cuddle. I graduated to a better paid, less rewarding Saturday job in the Lotus Shoe Shop, and then became a waitress at the Merrythought Café (morning coffee, lunches and high teas served), where I learned to consume a sponge pudding with custard at speed while manoeuvring a tray of six more puddings up the stairs to the upper restaurant.

Love of books

My father was a chartered accountant but, in his own words, not really suited to it. He moved from accountancy into publishing, which he was extremely good at. He worked for Encyclopaedia Britannica and then as Managing Director of Caxton Publishing (who published educational books including Chambers Encyclopaedias) until Robert Maxwell bought the parent company and sacked all the MDs. My father eventually won his appeal for unfair dismissal and spent ten impecunious but very happy years running the Horsham Bookshop, selling second-hand books in the days before the internet, until his untimely death aged 62. I owe him many things, including my love of books, an understanding that the only way to succeed is to work hard, and (eventually) not to take myself too seriously.

After leaving school (we won't talk about my A-levels), I got a job as Assistant Matron at the Prebendal School, Chichester, the choir school for Chichester Cathedral. Assistant Matron sounds grand; it wasn't. There was lots of bed-making, darning socks, folding laundry, serving meals, doling out plasters and cough mixture and comforting homesick little boys. They were similar ages to my two younger brothers: I hope I was kind to them.

It was during an outbreak of chicken pox at the school that I decided I had a calling to nurse sick children. I applied and was accepted to train as a nurse at the Hospital for Sick Children, Great Ormond Street (GOS). Fortunately for me, the October 1973 intake was one of the last where A-levels were not mandatory.

Being an NHS Chief Executive

I finished at Prebendal in July 1973 with a summer to fill, so I got a job as a nursing assistant on one of the children's ward at Forest Hospital in Horsham, where I first encountered people who have learning disabilities. The hospital was a revelation and had a profound effect on how I think about the care of vulnerable people, and what equal opportunities really mean.

GOS was also a revelation.

I don't know what I was expecting, but it was nothing like the Prebendal sick bay. I was distressed by the horrific illnesses and disabilities of the children and felt useless and terrified about responding to their needs.

I covered this with bravado. It was a great deal harder and sadder than I had anticipated, and I spent a lot of time crying in secret. I now know that quite a few of the other student nurses were unhappy too, but there seemed to be a conspiracy of silence never to talk about it. I recall one or two of our tutors trying to broach the subject of what it meant emotionally to look after sick and dying children, with little success. What seemed to get us through was appearing efficient and blasé, never talking about our feelings and instead becoming as knowledgeable as we could, as quickly as we could, about diseases, syndromes and treatments.

That and partying, for which I was renowned.

October 1973: Hospital for Sick Children, Great Ormond Street, Integrated State Registered and Registered Sick Children's Nursing Set (That's me, second row from the bottom on the far right)

The course lasted three years and eight months, including a year at Addenbrooke's Hospital, Cambridge and three months at Queen Charlotte's Maternity Hospital, London. I had to complete an additional three months because, early on when I was unhappy, I was inclined to take days off sick for spurious reasons, and was then hoist with my own petard when I needed knee surgery, thereby exceeding the maximum number of days we were allowed to miss. I qualified three months after my friends, in October 1977.

Prince Charles

GOS held two graduation ceremonies a year. Chair of the board of governors, Lady Callaghan, wife of then prime minister Jim Callaghan, was always joined by a celebrity to give out the prizes. For my colleagues in the October 1973 set, it was veteran DJ David Jacobs. Because I qualified three months later than them, I was put into a different graduation ceremony where we had an upgrade, and HRH Prince Charles was the celebrity. But I refused to go without my friends. I always felt bad about denying my mother the chance to see me shake the hand of royalty. I hope I eventually made up for it in January 2013 when she saw me collect my CBE from Prince Charles.

We qualified as state registered general nurses (SRNs) and registered sick children's nurses (RSCNs) with an obstetrics certificate that reduced by six months the time it would take to become midwives, should we choose to do this.

I loved and hated my nurse training in equal measure. I would not have survived for four years had it not been for my parents; they were proud of me and I didn't want to let them down, as I felt I had in other ways. There were also my dear friends, four of whom remain very close. They think it is hilarious that the naughtiest girl in the hospital went on to become a chief executive.

How I learned that being in hospital can be bad for you

While I was working at Chesterton, a hospital for the elderly on the outskirts of Cambridge, I had the opportunity to spend a day with the geriatric health visitor, a potential misnomer as she wasn't geriatric – just her patients. She had stylish clothes, a cream Morris Traveller, and a dear little cocker spaniel. We went to visit a lady who I recalled previously in hospital lying incontinent in bed with her face turned to the wall. When we arrived at her cottage, she hobbled to the door to let us in, all smiles, and ushered us into a cosy kitchen where she made us a cup of tea while her cat dozed on the windowsill. It was a seminal moment as I realised that being in hospital could actually be bad for people.

I stayed on as a staff nurse at GOS for a few months, and was just beginning to get the measure of it. But my ambition was to get out of hospital work and become a health visitor. I secured a place to train at Brighton Polytechnic in September 1978, which meant a move back to Sussex. To fill in, I got a staff nurse post at Chailey Heritage, another semi-closed institution, this one for children with profound physical disabilities.

At 23, I was one of the youngest health visitors ever to qualify. I do sometimes wonder how much help I was as I gave my earnest, evidence-based advice to women, often considerably older and more experienced in life than me. I had a second stint at health visiting after practising on my own children, and I think I did it with more compassion and less zeal the second time. As I still live in Brighton, I sometimes bump into parents who I long ago advised about breastfeeding or nappy rash, and mothers I attempted to support as they struggled through postnatal depression and slowly learned to love their babies. They are always very nice about my efforts.

During the health visitor course, I also found that I enjoyed the discipline of studying full-time. It gave me a hankering for the concentrated academic experience of a university degree. Increasingly, I grew to feel I had deprived myself of this the first time around.

So, after much soul-searching and financial calculation, aged 27 I left my health visitor job and acquired a place at the University of Sussex as what was then considered to be a mature undergraduate student. I chose to study social psychology, one of my best ever decisions. Our daughter was born at the end of the first year, an even better decision, so I intermitted for a year to stay at home and look after her, returning to university when she was aged one and could go to the wonderful university crèche. I became pregnant again in my third year and graduated when I was 7 months pregnant. So, what with marriage, a 2:1 and two babies, university was a life-changing experience.

University of Sussex

Another good decision was to go back to the University of Sussex from 1995 – 1996 to take a part-time master's degree in public sector management. My husband Steve is more financially prudent than me; when he saw how many books I had invested in for the Masters course, he decided that to get full value for them, he would do the same course. Except he got a better mark than me. In part to show our appreciation to Sussex, I served on the Council of the university from 2009 until 2015. I will always be a huge supporter of my alma mater.

Being an NHS Chief Executive

After our son was born in September 1986, I stayed at home with the children for another year, with the occasional night shift at the local children's hospital to keep my hand in and help pay the bills. The need to replenish our pitiful bank balance, and for me to have an occasional cup of coffee without a small child permanently attached, led me back to health visiting, part time, for another four years. I still have my financial calculations for that period: monthly salary after deductions, £400; childcare, £300. It was worth going to work, but these sums explain why I opted out of re-joining the NHS Pension Scheme for a number of years – something I regret rather a lot now.

My move into management was unplanned. I was a union rep and sat on the other side of the table from managers in meetings and at disciplinary hearings. I was seriously impressed by some, such as David Bowden, the District General Manager, who exuded positivity and composure and always made time in meetings to encourage views from the people who didn't say as much as the more vocal members.

But I was less impressed by others. I remember a manager telling me what she did when she received a memo from a member of staff. (I had just sent her one about a serious leak in the roof at the clinic where I worked, which was in a converted garage.) She said that she put all her memos in a drawer, unanswered, and waited to see if the person raised the matter again. Apparently, if it was really important, they would. Some people appear to use the same system nowadays. Obviously, we all get far too many emails, but for those awaiting an urgent reply, such an approach is deeply frustrating.

Life before email

There was no email in those days. Memos had to be typed with a carbon copy kept for your file. If you were lucky, someone who could type properly would do it for you, but if not, you did it yourself using one finger of each hand, and working extremely slowly because any mistake was permanent. Then you either used one of your precious allocation of postage stamps, or put your missive into the internal post bag that was collected three times a week but could be rather haphazard on delivery dates, if it arrived at all. For anything urgent or really important, you dropped it off at its destination by hand.

A chance encounter with a health visitor colleague gave me the nudge to dip my toe into the exciting but choppy waters of NHS management. One Friday, a day I didn't usually work, I popped in briefly to our offices for a meeting. As we were leaving, she asked me if I was going to apply for the Community Nurse Manager post in Lewes that had been recently advertised.

I hadn't given such a move even a thought. But her question sent me into a turmoil. I had actually been considering a career change, and had been idly exploring the possibility of re-training as a lawyer. But my heart just wasn't in it: I loved the NHS.

And so I found myself going home and with trembling fingers, dialling the office of the Director of Nursing. She was out. It was already the closing date; it looked like game over. But her secretary, who knew me, said that she was sure the director would be pleased to receive my application first thing on Monday.

This was 1990. My husband Steve, at the time a science teacher and lifelong computer geek, had bought us an Amstrad computer for use at home, plus a rudimentary dot-matrix printer. I spent all weekend on my application and delivered it personally, with shaking hands, first thing on Monday morning. It may have been the comparatively polished finish of that application, or the professional-looking overhead projector slides I used at my interview, also courtesy of Steve, that got me the job.

Or perhaps they thought that it was time I tried life on the other side of the table?

Having accepted the post, I was filled with terror. I was moving from working three days a week in a job I loved and knew well, to a full-time position doing something I knew next to nothing about. From managing no-one but myself and a nursing assistant (who in truth managed me) I was to be responsible for 100 staff, with no management training. And I didn't even know where the Lewes office was.

I had some sleepless nights, standing watch over the children as they slept, and weeping because I believed I was abandoning them. In truth, between primary school, our lovely part-time nanny, Steve and my parents, they were going to be more than fine. One of my dilemmas was that I had decided I wanted to continue to take them to school myself two days a week and always collect them on Tuesday afternoons. How was I going to achieve it? Those were still the days when women would get asked at interview whether they had a family and told that if they did, to please make sure it didn't interfere with their work. And although that hadn't happened to me, I was determined to be a woman who juggled without it showing.

I could write a whole book about those first two years, as no doubt could the nurses on the receiving end of my early management skills. We had some extraordinary times. I learned about the ingenuity of district nurses, what rural poverty means, and the horrors of leg ulcers, terminal arthritis and morbid obesity. I also learned how wonderful it can be to be supported to die in your own bed at home, without pain because the nurse knows how to set up a syringe driver and make a bed cradle out of a cut-up cardboard box and some pillows to keep you comfortable, with your family and/or beloved pets around you.

I also became acquainted with the differences between cottage and teaching hospitals, that school nurses do a great deal more than checking for nits, and that health visitors who do their own thing are more alarming to their managers than I had appreciated when I was a bit of a maverick health visitor myself.

One of my early management failures

I said earlier I went from managing myself and a nursing assistant to 100 staff. Fifty-five of the staff worked in an NHS nursing home, 20 were health visitors and school nurses, one was my amazing secretary who also managed our clinic building, and the remaining 24 were district nurses – sisters, staff nurses and nursing auxiliaries.

These 24 kind and skilful women shared a small office on the ground floor of the clinic above the boiler room that nowadays would not even be considered an acceptable space for two people. The team covered shifts seven days a week from 7 am – 8 pm. For whole team meetings we would book the large clinic room, but first thing every morning there were at least ten of them crammed together in the tiny office, perched on desks or two to a chair as they planned their visits for the day.

I offered a swap with my office, because it was cooler and airier, but it was no larger and being upstairs was less convenient for carrying equipment in and out. For two years I sought a new office for them, and they never grumbled about my lack of success. What impressed them less was that I asked them to remove the old wooden commode that they kept in the office

> *for any patient who might need one in an emergency and which otherwise served as an extra office chair. It smelt and seemed to me both unhygienic and not very nice.*
>
> *They eventually obliged, but I discovered later that the offending item was simply relocated to live in the back of one of their cars. It is probably a valuable antique by now.*

I also found out what it was like to be managed by someone with male chauvinist tendencies who bullied those who showed signs of weakness. I won't name this person, but one of his favourite sayings was 'Don't come to me with problems, come to me with solutions' – one of the stupidest things I have ever heard. I was his favourite, and yet I would get a sick feeling in my stomach when I saw his car in the car park, and worked out a route to get to my little room upstairs without having to pass his more palatial office suite.

One of my colleagues was so concerned about making a good impression that, before meetings with him, she would get her hairdresser to come to her house at the crack of dawn to do her hair and make-up. This ploy didn't work, and she was often close to tears by the end of our monthly management team meetings after yet another intellectual mauling by a person who thought it was witty to drink from a mug with 'The Boss' written on it. I tried to be sympathetic, but I found her exasperating - she could have spent her early mornings more usefully going through her budget statements. I wish I had been kinder, and helped her more.

Learning from experience

People think competition in the NHS is a relatively new thing. But there have always been people who set one person against another, or indeed one organisation against another, to create a 'healthy' contest. In 1993, the community and mental health trust where I worked was asked to compete against its sister acute trust to replace a small local hospital with a polyclinic. My trust 'won', and I was allocated the responsibility to lead the building project. I remember asking what a polyclinic was and was told by someone very senior: 'I don't f***ing know, just build us one.'

Which I did, with a lot of help and some considerable hindrance from people who couldn't accept that the new building could be better than what it replaced. And more by luck than judgement on my part. The architect, Brian Graham of Nightingale Associates, and I clicked when he asked me to write an ethos statement. Hove Polyclinic turned out really well and has won many design awards. People remark on its beauty and utility to this day. If you are managing your first building project, there are many places to look for guidance. For me, William Morris offers the wisest counsel:

'Have nothing in your house that you do not know to be useful, or believe to be beautiful.'

The building projects we NHS managers leave behind will outlast our careers, possibly our lives. It feels wrong, to me, to leave anything behind that is not both beautiful AND useful. With Hove Polyclinic, I was lucky to have achieved that.

After the community services joined the mental health services and became South Downs Health NHS Trust in 1992, there was a reorganisation which favoured me, especially as I found myself acting up almost immediately when my manager went on maternity leave. Another reorganisation the following year led to a more senior job, and another, and by 1995 I had been appointed Director of Nursing with a place on the trust board. I had an illuminating and mainly wonderful time learning to be an executive director until 2000, during which time the term *clinical governance* was introduced in the NHS and a predecessor of the Care Quality Commission, the Commission for Health Improvement, was created.

During that final year I realised that, having been a late starter into management, if I ever wanted to become a chief executive myself, I needed to get some experience elsewhere. My generous chair and chief executive agreed to my secondment, first to be Emergency Care Director for the South East of England, and then to be Project Director setting up West Sussex Health and Social Care NHS Trust, one of the predecessor trusts to Sussex Partnership. I decided to apply for the chief executive position during that second secondment, for reasons I will explain later. I was appointed on 20 December 2001.

The things I learned along the way, from then until 2014, are what this book is about.

Chapter 2

Choosing the job and then getting it

When I was first thinking about applying for a chief executive (CE) post, I was given a wonderful piece of advice by Andy Horne, my boss at the time. Andy was an honourable and funny colleague. He said something like this, just a bit more colourfully:

'Lisa, you are going to get an NHS chief executive job. There are good jobs and some that are not so good. Just make sure you get one that you really want.'

Surprisingly, many people simply don't work this out for themselves. If Andy hadn't given this advice to me, I could have been one of them. Let me explain.

People think of the NHS as one huge organisation. To some extent it is in that the majority of us who work in it or use it share the same values about high-quality health care for all when needed, no matter what contributions people have personally paid. But having worked in a number of parts of the NHS, I know, as I'm sure you will, that all parts are not equal and things are not done in the same way everywhere.

Another useful piece of advice came from my chair at Sussex Partnership, John Bacon CB. John is a wise owl who sat at the top of the NHS for a number of years, managing to maintain his reputation for being tough and clever while remaining a thoroughly nice bloke. John says that people have very short memories. At one minute before midnight, as the new leader, you are the knight in shining armour, galloping in to the rescue. But at one minute past, everything that happens or has ever happened is your responsibility. Here are my thoughts on the kind of things you might want to think about as you make your decision on what job(s) to apply for. They are entirely unscientific.

Types of organisations

One way to help you make your decision is to consider the type of organisation you would like to become accountable for running. The majority of people in the NHS work in trusts, and so this is where you will find most chief executive jobs. At the time of writing, there are 256 trusts in total, with 158 having achieved a greater, albeit increasingly limited, ability to govern their own affairs by becoming foundation trusts (FTs). The 'pipeline' for becoming an FT (how we love to misuse the English language by making-up words and creating acronyms) has pretty much dried up at the moment; whether it will be unblocked any day soon seems unlikely, given the tough economic climate and the nervousness of the regulators Monitor, now part of NHS Improvement, and the Care Quality Commission (CQC) after what happened at Mid Staffordshire NHS Foundation Trust. Cost-cutting in pursuit of FT status was cited in an independent report about failings resulting in patient deaths at Stafford hospital between 2005-2009.

One of the things you will need to consider is whether you have your heart set on running a trust that has already achieved FT status. There are no guarantees that it will maintain the status, but you will almost certainly lose your job if it goes into special measures. Or do you want to risk your reputation leading the bid for your trust to become an FT, or whatever the next iteration is going to be called. This was hard enough in 2008 when I did it, but must be many times more so today. Not an easy choice, but you need to make it with your eyes open.

There is one further option, which is running a trust with no obvious future, and therefore you would be overseeing its demise in some way, through merger, acquisition or break up. This is not a role for the faint-hearted, and is rarely sufficiently recognised as being extremely hard work mentally and emotionally. In my view, it is only something that a really experienced chief executive should take on. There is also a tendency for CEs and chairs to be appointed to such roles, get there, and then spend the next few years trying to prove that those who thought the trust wasn't viable were wrong. Occasionally this succeeds; more frequently sadly not.

The taxonomy of trust types can be divided again into what trusts do, although these boundaries are becoming increasingly blurred. There are the large acute teaching trusts; these are seen as plum jobs which go to high fliers who have already proved themselves and, I note simply as a matter of fact, are still almost always men. There are then a range of other acute trusts, some with and some without other associated services, of varying sizes. There are the specialist trusts, which tend to have fared very well in past years but are finding the new commissioning arrangements rather more of a challenge. There are ambulance trusts, ten in total, with five who have achieved foundation status. And there are community trusts, which are relatively new because they grew from the demise of the now defunct primary care trusts.

At the time of writing, only a small number of these community trusts have achieved foundation status. Some are instead exploring interesting new models such as becoming social enterprises with various types of staff ownership schemes.

And there are the specialist mental health trusts, such as Sussex Partnership, 52 in total at the time of writing. Some of these have started taking on other services, particularly in the community, in a few cases more than doubling their size, with some very good outcomes for patients and staff, some less so.

And then there are non-NHS organisations, falling into two broad categories, for-profit and not-for-profit, although again this boundary feels increasingly blurred, as charities can set up subsidiary companies. And finally, there are joint ventures, which can be quasi-organisations set up between NHS FTs and other non-statutory bodies.

Providing or commissioning?

People who work on the commissioning side of the NHS have a tendency to call the above organisations 'providers'. I don't think it is intended to be insulting, but it can feel a somewhat dismissive term when one is on the receiving end of it. There are commissioners who prefer never to use the name of the trust from whom they commission services, and either call them 'the provider' or reduce their name to an unagreed acronym. They may not realise it, but this is a power thing. Which isn't surprising, because commissioning is extremely difficult, with limited resources, and usually has to be done with a great deal less knowledge and information than the providers hold. The results are less tangible, more long term and it is harder to see the impact than in direct service provision.

Running an NHS commissioning organisation is also extremely challenging because in my opinion, shared I know by others, the goalposts get moved far too frequently. Whatever political parties say before elections, there appear to be none that can resist reorganising commissioning once they have been elected. And then there are the management-driven reorganisations that occur in between. In the 17 years since I became an NHS chief executive, there have been six reorganisations of the commissioning side of the NHS, and there are undoubtedly more to come.

Some people love working in the relatively new Clinical Commissioning Groups (CCGs), because at long last clinicians are leading decisions about the care of patients. But others find it frustrating because decision-making can be laborious and time-consuming, and the rules are difficult to navigate and full of legal pitfalls. There is an inbuilt tension because general practitioner (GP) members of CCGs are also, by definition, providers of primary health care services. Thus, they are not legally allowed to commission major changes to primary care themselves, which arguably is the part of the NHS that needs to expand and develop most. This is being tested in some places and will almost certainly have to change.

Finally, there are the Sustainability and Transformation Partnerships (STPs), 44 at the time of writing, which have been set up to bring together the different parts of the NHS and social care system and try to get everyone to reach decisions which are for the collective good. I have no direct experience of STPs, as they were only just being invented as I left. They seem like a very good idea in principle, but from what I hear, they provide interesting conundrums in accountability plus pressure from elected members and other stakeholders. All of the above relates only to the English NHS. One of the effects of devolution is that commissioning in Scotland, Northern Ireland and Wales is done differently, with no clear separation between commissioners and providers.

I don't know enough about top-level roles in organisations such as shared service providers, commissioning support units or the independent sector equivalents to say anything particularly helpful, but they each need running and there will be an accountable officer in every case. If you are interested in one of these roles, and have the right set of skills, these are jobs where new ground can undoubtedly be broken.

Regulators and other national bodies

Apart from NHS England, NHS Improvement (formed from Monitor and the Trust Development Authority) and the Care Quality Commission, there are a number of other national bodies, each of which have executive and non-executive roles, including Public Health England, Health Education England, the National Institute for Clinical Excellence (NICE) and the NHS Leadership Academy, although again, there are changes afoot as I write, with the Leadership Academy being subsumed into Health Education England. It is unlikely you would be considering a top-level role in one of these if you don't already know a great deal about what they do.

Nonetheless, if you are applying for any leadership role in today's NHS, you do need to understand who does what within all of these bodies, where you can go for help, and where challenges will come from.

Doing your homework

This leads me on to homework, or due diligence as people now like to call it. Having decided what type of organisation you would like to run, you will have started looking at jobs. These days, many public sector chief executive jobs are filled using head-hunters, although a few are still simply advertised in the *Health Service Journal*, the *Guardian* or the NHS Jobs website. This gives you an indication of how wide the board and governors are spreading the net, and therefore whether they already have a preferred candidate in mind.

But never assume anything. One of the biggest lessons I learned during my years as an NHS chief executive is that far more happens by error or omission than people would have you believe.

The best advice I can give you is to find out as much as you can. DO NOT simply rely on websites or published accounts. Talk to as many people as possible. The purpose is not to impress them, but to find things out. So be in listening mode. Leave time and enough space for them to tell you things that you haven't asked.

And remember that the head-hunter is your friend. They will not want to recommend you for a job that won't suit you because it will impact on their reputation. At the same time, they want their search to produce an appointment, because their fee structure is skewed to a successful outcome, so talk honestly to them and let them help you prepare.

These are the questions I would want answered before getting anywhere near an interview:

- Why is your potential predecessor leaving/has already left?
- What do the available published reports tell you?
- Is this organisation really viable? (*Hint:* the problems at Mid Staffordshire NHS Foundation Trust almost certainly grew from a very big question mark about viability, given the trust's proximity to larger teaching organisations, difficulty in recruiting and retaining high calibre staff, and medium-term problems with financial viability as a foundation trust in a more hostile commissioning world. The eventual decision to merge it with a larger teaching organisation supports this view)
- What will it be like to work with the trust chair? Can you develop a good chemistry? Do you share the same values? Can you laugh at the same things?
- What are relations with non-executive directors, staff representatives, governors, commissioners, other partners, elected members, regulators, the public, local media and most importantly patient groups like? There will always be room for improvement, but beware those who want to cast the new chief executive in a knight in shining army role. The only way from that is down.
- Can you work with at least some of the existing executive team? If not, why not? Beware of creating a coup; they rarely end well.
- Where and how can you truly add value? In other words, does the board want radical development and change, just some change or mainly more of the same? And are they right? Only you will know which answer is the right one for you. Replacing someone who is viewed to have done a great job might be harder than following someone who is seen to have 'failed'. At the same time, beware the fickle board who are 'out with the old and in with the new'. It may not be too long before you become the old yourself.

Please also give very careful consideration to what my previous coach and now friend Lollie Tuckey of Huntwood Associates calls 'hygiene factors'. These are far more important than some people think. And if you haven't resolved them to your satisfaction, you will almost certainly give this away by showing some unintended diffidence during the interview process.

- What area does this organisation serve? If it isn't somewhere you already know, can you develop an honest and deep affinity with it?
- If you plan to move, where will you live? And how will your partner/children/parents/friends/cat cope with the change?
- If you are going to commute, is the journey to work bearable? If not, can you make it so?
- If you are going to stay away from home in the week, as an increasing number of senior leaders do, can you manage with this? Will it make you unhappy? If yes, can you mitigate it?
- Can you honestly see yourself staying here for a considerable time, say five years? This is an important question. You may think of it as a two or three year job and a stepping-stone to something more exciting, but that may not happen, and more importantly it almost certainly won't be the right thing for the organisation or you.
- Would you feel proud if you got the job? Would it make your heart sing?

Getting the job

Having done all your homework and made your decision about whether to apply, you are three quarters of the way there. No doubt you will remember all the times you have sat on the opposite side of the interview table, and what you did and didn't like about people you have interviewed. The most important thing at this point, however, is simply to **be the best version of yourself**. Having given yourself this chance, you can then afford to let nature take its course. If I were writing a true self-help book, I would repeat the phrase **be the best version of yourself** many times. It is the most important piece of advice anyone can give you.

Your application has more purpose than just getting you an interview. It is where you will distil all your homework into a précis, pull together some conclusions to present to those drawing up the shortlist, and give yourself a basis for the interview process itself.

It is extraordinary that people applying for top-level jobs often write poor applications. But they do. This may be due to lack of practice. Make sure yours is excellent - succinct, in perfect English, in a standard readable sized font, with absolutely no typos or other mistakes - and check that it fulfils the requirements set out. If you are asked to provide a maximum two-sided CV, and yours is longer, get some help trimming it down. If it runs to more than two sides it is probably too long anyway. If you are asked to write a letter explaining why you want the job, do so. Avoid being overly informal, name-dropping or using acronyms without explaining what they mean. Get the name of your potential employer organisation exactly right. And flatter your audience by showing you have done your homework about their key priorities, achievements and challenges. Less is usually more, but if you know you are inclined to excessive brevity, remember that people can't read your mind. Especially on paper.

Assuming your excellent application has led to you being shortlisted, there are some more dos, don'ts and maybes prior to the interview process itself. One of the questions many people ask is whether to make personal contact with the chair. I cannot imagine any appointing officer being offended by a shortlisted candidate getting in touch prior to interview, even if you have already met or spoken with each other. If you are unsure, please enquire – you do not want the chair to make a negative judgement because you haven't been in touch.

If you do manage to speak to the chair, again be in listening mode. This conversation is not part of the interview, but you can reduce your chances of success if you start setting out your stall before you know what they are looking for.

Getting in touch with other members of the panel, unless you know them already or have been asked to do so, is, in my view, probably a no-no. It may not be intended, but it could look like lobbying.

The interview process

By all means do as much preparation for the interview as you feel you need. But do not over-prepare. It is, after all, a conversation rather than a bravura performance.

The same applies to any focus groups that have been set up. You should not dominate the conversation; show respect and listen carefully to those who have given up their time to be there, and use what you have learned to help you in any subsequent groups and the formal part of the interview.

If you know anyone or even everyone on the panel, you run the risk of two things:

- Overfamiliarity and/or the inappropriate use of in-jokes, which should be avoided at all costs
- Assuming the panel know about things you have done, and therefore not mentioning them or failing to use them to illustrate your points.

The best thing to do in these circumstances is to try to pretend to yourself that you really don't know any of them. You may be worried about telling them things they already know; the chances are that they won't have the details of the examples you are using anyway. Give yourself the benefit of the doubt and tell them. Most of us in any case like to hear about something we already know a bit about; it can be strangely reassuring.

Dame Ruth Carnall gave me some brilliant advice about how not to be nervous (or as nervous) in an interview for a senior job. She said that it is up to the interviewee to put the panel at their ease. They will be as anxious as you are, possibly more so, because they want to make the right decision and there will be much riding on them doing so. Your job is to give them confidence so that they can make that right decision, and hopefully choose you.

You may get the first chief executive job you go for. But you probably won't. In my case, practice made perfect. Because I had a self-inflicted, unpleasant experience of making a complete hash of it the first time, I approached my next attempt like a military exercise, including getting fit mentally and physically. You may not need to drop a stone by reacquainting yourself with regular exercise and eschewing alcohol and chocolate. But getting a new haircut and choosing something smart and flattering to wear will definitely help.

It will help you even more to spend time away from the hubbub of your current job so you can prepare thoughtfully and thoroughly. You truly owe this time to yourself and your potential new organisation.

Practice makes perfect

Dame Ruth Carnall was my boss at the NHS South East Regional office in 2000/2001. She was wonderful, but the job I was seconded to was extremely stressful, and I neglected myself during that period. Towards the end of the secondment, I had either to go back to my old job as a director of nursing or find something else that suited me.

Ruth's advice about applying for new jobs was excellent, although I didn't apply it very well on my first attempt. I was being interviewed one Friday in April 2001 for a project director job running one of the putative West Sussex PCTs. I hated how I

(Practice makes perfect cont.)

looked and what I was wearing for the interview. I felt fat and frumpy.

Worse, I knew I was ill-prepared and uninspired. And as if to prove it, halfway through the interview, which was already going badly, my phone rang in my bag. I scrabbled to switch it off and gasped 'I'm so sorry, that's terrible.' To which Candy Morris CBE, who was interviewing me, replied 'Yes, it is.'

With hindsight, my heart wasn't in it. I spent that weekend hiding under the bedclothes. And then on Monday, I faced my humiliation and emailed Candy with apologies for my abject performance. A month later I was in front of her again for another project job application which went rather better. That second project enabled me to make the decision to prepare and apply for the chief executive post, which I eventually got.

Having sat on quite a few chief executive interview panels as an external assessor or non-executive director, I have developed my own thoughts on what comes over well and not so well from candidates. If you haven't had such an opportunity, ask around and see if you can get some experience, perhaps by sitting in on a focus group. It may not be possible but it would be hugely valuable before you find yourself in that chair.

The final thing to remember is that getting the job is just page 1, chapter 1. Please make sure you have plenty of energy left. I hope you will read the rest of my book, but I hope even more that one day you will get enough experience to write a book of your own.

Being an NHS Chief Executive

Why I really chose my job

Let me let you into a secret. I had a very specific reason for choosing to apply for the chief executive job in West Sussex back in 2001, and then to continue the work I had started and become chief executive of the new combined trust in 2006. It goes all the way back to 1973, when I was 18, and working over the summer at the Forest Hospital (see Chapter 1). The 26 children on Highbeech 2, the ward to which I was allocated, were all profoundly disabled. Some had conditions they were born with, such as microcephaly (where the skull and brain are abnormally small and underdeveloped) or autism. Some had acquired conditions caused by oxygen starvation at birth, including severe cerebral palsy and other unspecified brain damage. And some had degenerative conditions that were not apparent at birth but which led to them becoming increasingly mentally and physically disabled. I can still remember every single child on that ward. I have thought about them all a great deal since, and hoped many times that I might meet some of them again.

Nurses shouldn't have favourites, but I was inexperienced and there was one little boy who became mine. He reminded me of my youngest brother because they were the same age and had similar pudding basin haircuts. But whereas that summer my brother was playing cricket, reading comics and having friends round for tea, this little chap had to wear a helmet because, despite being on very strong medication, he had frequent fits. He also had no sense of danger and a very short attention span. He loved his food but forgot he was being fed unless you held him firmly in your lap, preferably singing nursery rhymes loudly at the same time. Like all the other children at the hospital, he was doubly incontinent. He would tear off nappies as soon as you put them on, so that he and those caring for him needed frequent cleaning up. The only recognisable sound he made was a distinctive guttural noise, which depending on frequency and volume could indicate happiness, sadness, pain or anger. One of the side effects of the drugs he needed to control his frequent seizures was extreme photosensitivity. He loved to run outside on the grass, but 1973 was a hot summer and he had to remain indoors. It was heart-breaking to see him rubbing his head on the window and crying to go out.

I had thought of this little boy off and on throughout the next 28 years. And then in 2001, on a visit as part of my orientation for the project director job, I met him again. He was now 40, still an NHS inpatient, living in a house with six other people who also had severe learning disabilities. I recognised him before I saw him, because of the sound he made. I like to think he recognised me too. But in truth I doubt it. People with learning disabilities get used to many people looking after them, and know how to spot a friendly face. After a bearlike hug, he dragged me off to show me his bedroom, music centre and photographs. I stayed for a while. It was very hard to say goodbye.

Roll forward a few years. One of the first difficulties I experienced as chief executive of the trust in West Sussex was persuading the local authority and the PCTs to understand that commissioning services for people with learning disabilities needed to reach a higher position than rock bottom of their priority list. This was particularly so in the north of West Sussex, where for historical reasons the income received by us for looking after people with complex needs was less than it would have cost for someone without any disabilities to live in a cheap bed and breakfast.

I remember having to make the case for two patients, both of whom had serious problems eating and were dangerously underweight, to be assessed by a dietician with a view to introducing tube feeding. It is well known that malnutrition in people with learning disabilities can cause great pain and suffering, as well as reducing life expectancy. It is unusual for chief executives to get involved in clinical care, but the staff had been given the run-around and I was eventually asked to intervene. I was initially told that because they lived in the care of my trust, they were ineligible to be seen by an NHS dietician, and that somehow we should find the money to purchase private treatment from the grossly inadequate fees we were paid. Suffice to say that I made sure they got the care they needed from the NHS. But it was not our commissioners' finest hour.

It seemed to me that the people concerned were being treated as non-citizens. Their status as long stay hospital inpatients meant they had no access to primary care or disability benefits, no choice of where or with whom they lived, and were too often missing out on many other things that most of us take for granted.

There were 168 such people in West Sussex in 2001. Our ambition was to help them all move on to their own homes, only sharing with one or two others if this was what they wanted, and achieving maximum independence with whatever support was needed to achieve this. This became known as The Place to Live project. As we set up the new Sussex Partnership, a larger trust with greater influence, one of our first priorities was to complete this project with West Sussex County Council, the PCTs and various specialist housing providers. The last person finally moved into their own home, and thus became a full citizen, in 2011. It still feels like one of our most significant achievements.

And the little boy who must now be a man in his 50s was amongst that group. I like to think of him living somewhere in his own home with people helping him do the things he finds fulfilling, including running in the garden and feeling the grass under his feet.

And that is why I chose my job.

Being an NHS Chief Executive

Chapter 3

On communication and social media

Introduction: taking advice

My first chair, Glynn Jones OBE, previously chief executive of Brighton and Hove City Council, gave me some salutary advice soon after we started working together. He said that whatever time and money you are planning to devote to communicating with your staff and the public, double it and it still won't be enough.

But that doesn't mean you should give up trying. You need to find people who are professional communicators, and then open yourself up to their advice, including making it easy for them to tell you what not to do.

Most leaders think they are good at receiving advice. Trust me, this isn't always so. We are, by virtue of what we do, strong characters. And we can hold strong views, tending to think we are right about most things. This combination can make it difficult to advise us. It is important to know this. Telling those in professional roles that we really do welcome their advice, despite how we may sometimes come across, is important too.

But the most crucial thing is actually listening to them, and being prepared to change our minds. I didn't do this all of the time. But when I did, it really helped.

I like to say I recruited my first Head of Communications on the number 26 bus. He says it was he who persuaded me that I needed a Head of Communications. Either way, I had known Andrew Partington and respected him for many years, first as a local journalist and then as Head of Communications at the Health Authority (remember those?). Our children went to the same schools, and we lived near each other, hence being on the same bus coming back from the shops one Saturday. We agreed to meet and he applied to work at West Sussex Health and Social Care NHS Trust (WSHSC), reporting directly to the newly appointed chief executive, me. We learned a lot together, and he certainly learned how to manage me.

Listening

In organisations spread across many sites like WSHSC, and latterly Sussex Partnership, communication can be rather more haphazard than where staff work in one large building, such as an acute hospital. There is a story that Sir Jonathan Michael, when he was chief executive of Guy's and St Thomas' NHS Foundation Trust, would stand on a small stool, the type used in operating theatres, and invite staff to gather round, soon attracting a crowd with whom to share his latest thoughts and hear their views. I asked him once if it was true, and he said sometimes! It sounds wonderful to be able to do this. Mind you, Sir Jonathan is a superb raconteur as well as a great leader, so you would want to listen to him anyway.

When we set up the trust in West Sussex, people – patients, staff, our partners and the public – thought the organisation was going to be huge. It was true that we would have over 100 sites, but most of these were quite small and isolated. The trust wasn't huge at all, just widely spread. I already knew that it wouldn't be long before we would have to reconsider our size in terms of ongoing viability.

Meanwhile, I felt that we needed to listen to the fears being expressed. Wherever meetings were held to consult on the proposals to set up the new trust, people said it was too far for someone to travel, or the wrong time of day, or had the wrong sort of parking or public transport links. We traipsed around some of the smallest and most out-of-the-way village halls and community centres imaginable, just because someone somewhere had said that if we didn't, we would offend someone else. Occasionally we gave the presentation about the new trust just to ourselves, which made the Question and Answer session nice and short, but was rather a waste of time and public money.

Whatever we did, there were people who seemed determined to take offence. I found myself promising that, during the first year after setting up the new trust, we would hold our public board meetings in a rotation of venues around West Sussex. This proved to be a logistical nightmare, with unforeseen expenses. So, at the end of that first year, we took the decision to hold all the meetings at our headquarters, advertise them well, make the agendas as accessible as possible and do everything we could to make those who attended feel welcome.

The truth can be stranger than fiction

Our first board meeting took place in a community hall in the north of West Sussex. There was to be a jumble sale at the same venue the following Saturday, and large piles of jumble were already being assembled, accompanied by a musty smell.

The meeting passed without incident. However, a week later we received a call from a lady who had attended. She had been staying with a friend prior to the meeting, and had accidentally left a nearly-new dressing gown in a plastic carrier bag underneath her chair. When she went back to reclaim it a few days later, she was horrified to find it had been sold with the jumble. We found ourselves refunding her £39.99 to buy a new one.

I stood by that. Communication is two-way, although quite a lot of leaders forget this and think it is all about getting the message across. This is why I think board meetings, fascinating though they may be for those involved, are a pretty terrible way to communicate. We can do so much better with open sessions which are more informal and where we can have real discussions with the attendees.

Books like *If They Haven't Heard It, You Haven't Said It* by Harvey Thomas and Roy Lilley were all the rage when I was learning to be a leader in the 1990s. They are very useful if you are having trouble getting a message across. However, good leadership is about engaging with people and developing ideas together, not simply telling them what you think.

Balloons

An idea that arose from meetings we had with patient and family groups during the set-up phase of the new West Sussex trust was to hold an introductory event at a venue in a village right in the centre of the county. No matter that it was almost equally inconvenient for everyone attending - at least we could hand on heart say that it was truly central.

We listened, and we held the event. To create a memorable closing session, it was agreed that we would all share our honest hopes and concerns for the new trust and what would make it different from previous arrangements. Someone thought it would be a good idea to write these thoughts onto cardboard tags, tie them to helium balloons and let them off into the autumn sunset. And so the day culminated in a mass release of balloons, which made everyone feel included and provided a nice photo-opportunity. It was less popular with equestrians.

We had phone calls from two people with similar tales of how the balloons had drifted into their fields and spooked their valuable horses. One horse was suspected of ingesting a burst balloon, and another had galloped away in fright and become tangled in barbed wire. I spoke to both owners and apologised

---

> *unreservedly for the distress caused, and asked them to send me the vet's bills so that I could reimburse them.*
>
> *The bad news was that I don't think they were receptive to my anti-stigma 'Mental Health is Everyone's Business' message. But the good news was that the bills never arrived.*
>
> **Memo to self: where possible, avoid ponies.**

Some pros and cons of communication

People who have never run public services assume that the media just print or broadcast everything you tell them. Sadly, they don't. True, they are always looking for stories, but media releases about staff doing excellent things or patients being pleased with their care just aren't newsworthy, even for the local media with much space to fill. They need an angle and a hook, and someone who is prepared to say something that will be interesting or controversial enough for others to read or listen to.

Or for something to have gone wrong. In mental health services, unless you work very hard, the only time you will hit the media will be when a patient has harmed themselves, or, more rarely, someone else. It doesn't matter how carefully you say that these events are rare, or try to contextualise, you will always risk sounding defensive.

My favourite book on communication and leadership is *How to Win Friends and Influence People* by Dale Carnegie, first published in 1936. The principles at the end of each chapter in the later editions are great summaries. They stand the test of time. Carnegie was an ethical man who made a lot of money. And he always credited his sources.

'The ideas I stand for are not mine. I borrowed them from Socrates. I swiped them from Chesterfield. I stole them from Jesus. And I put them in a book. If you don't like their rules, whose would you use?'

I agree with him. There is no need to reinvent the wheel. But we have the advantages of the internet, email and social media. Carnegie would have had fun with these.

When I became a manager in 1990, the community nurses hated computers. Inputting data was time-consuming in those early years; you had to drive back to the office and then wait for a terminal to become free. Logging on and inputting your activity was laborious, and the computers seemed to give nothing back. In fact, it was worse than this. The information that the nurses input to Comcare, our IT system at the time, provided some rudimentary caseload information which managers then used to see which staff were working the hardest, and with which to set a standard for the others. But there was no complexity measurement. Activity was based on nothing but numbers.

The nurses also hated the mobile phones I organised for them so that they could keep in touch with each other to discuss patients or pick up new cases.

We covered a large area and I wanted to find a way that reduced unnecessary journeys. It was essentially about saving time. But I also wanted to be able to say that they were the first team in England to have mobile phones. To be honest, I never really knew if this was true. And the phones were admittedly pretty horrible. In 1991, to get a decent sized battery that lasted more than an hour, the mobile phone looked like an old army field telephone and weighed about 4 kg. The nurses resented having to lug one of these things around on top of all their other equipment. And I don't blame them – in our largely rural area, mobile phone masts were rare, so there were many places with no signal anyway.

Being an NHS Chief Executive

It is hard to imagine life now without mobile phones, texts, emails, search engines, blogging and social media, and the massive computing power of neat, flat devices that slide into our pockets, more powerful than mainframe computers of just a few years earlier. The first touchscreen smartphones came onto the market in 2007. In 2018, 80 per cent of people in the UK have one, and this is growing daily.

When I became a Chief Executive, email had already started taking over our lives. I would get about 50 emails a day. And because we wanted to know what was happening at all times, and there were to be no BlackBerrys or other such devices for another couple of years, we set up remote connections using ISDN lines. This meant that if someone wanted to call you at home or make contact with staff at an outlying centre or clinic, they often couldn't get through because the line was being used for data transfer. This is one of hundreds of examples we can all think of where something that was meant to make communication better had the opposite effect.

When I retired from Sussex Partnership, my emails had increased to around 200 a day. This was partly because of the post Mid-Staffordshire report and the growing concern about accountability. After the much-maligned NHS reorganisation in 2012 (see Chapter 6), there was a multiplication of different departments of commissioners, regulators and others whose job it is to hold NHS trusts to account. And people seem, truly, to have come to believe that sending an email to the accountable officer ensures it gets read and/or passed on to the right person, while providing an audit trail to prove that it had been sent, should this ever be needed by auditors or the Public Accounts Committee (the independent parliamentary group that holds those in public office to account). Email lists of people in jobs like mine are frequently sold, so you also get sales pitches for conferences and risk management products and services. Scam emails are also increasingly common.

But amongst all this clutter and noise, there will be emails from someone making a really worrying complaint, a commissioner who isn't happy about an aspect of a service, a member of staff who is trying to blow the whistle, or a missive from NHS Improvement or the CQC that if missed could be career limiting. Managing the inbox has become a major part of running the chief executive (CE) office.

When I first became a CE, I used to write an all-staff email each Christmas, with some end of year thoughts and my good wishes to everyone. I added a summer message a year or so later. In 2009, I started writing blogs on our intranet. And in 2010 I committed to writing a weekly personal public message, which went on our website. I promised that I would read and reply to all responses.

For me, this was a positive decision. I wrote every one myself, over 400 in total. It felt like a good weekly discipline[1] to reflect on what had happened in the past seven days and to illustrate this with examples. Writing them myself acted as an aide memoire for me about what had been happening, and allowed me to signal my increasing concern about, for example, the growing pressure on our staff and beds as the impact of the downturn began to have a negative effect on patients in ever increasing ways. Members of my executive team helped me decide on some of the broad content so that key messages about service pressures or change were reiterated and supported. Writing them also allowed me to share more of myself. I have re-read them in preparation for the book, and I notice they became more relaxed and open over the years.

Were they useful to staff, patients and the public? I would like to think so. But I am aware of the plethora of stuff that staff who work in public services such as the NHS are expected to read. I remember talking to a manager in my final months at Sussex Partnership. She said she liked to get in early and 'deal' with her emails. This made

---

[1] It was the idea of Councillor Sylvia Tidy, at the time chair of the East Sussex County Council Health Overview and Scrutiny Committee. She said she liked the weekly email that a colleague, chief executive wrote, and wondered if I might do the same. She had obviously read How to Win Friends and Influence People!

me feel really sad. For many managers, 'dealing' with an email means reading it, and if it seems important, writing a covering note and forwarding it with the original to others for them to read and take appropriate action. Emails are a very good way of creating work, and giving the appearance of being busy.

But they are not really work; they are just about work. They can get in the way of the real work of looking after patients and supporting staff. My weekly messages were meant to be my version of Sir Jonathan Michael grabbing a stool and chatting with staff. But I suspect that reading them might have felt like just another chore to our overworked staff.

Social Media

And so, to social media, and specifically, the pros and cons of developing a social media presence if you do a job like mine. I have a number of people to thank for introducing me to social media, particularly the wise Ann Grain from JAG Press and Publicity who helped me in 2010 to show who I really am via my communications. Ranjeet Kaile, our Head of Marketing and Communications, very subtly and skilfully helped me realise that I needed the help of someone like Ann. And Emily Sands, who worked with Ranjeet and showed me that social media and blogging are just another way of communicating.

The rules are the same as for all communications. I have written a couple of pieces about it, which at the time of writing are still available online[2]. In short, be yourself, be kind, try to be interesting, never post a comment in anger or under the influence of alcohol, and try not to be too up yourself.

---

[2] See Social Media for NHS Dummies HSJ 9 August 2012, and Why You Should be Persuading Your CEO and Senior Executives to Take to Twitter, Association for Healthcare Communications and Marketing blogs, October 2012

If you find yourself with a stalker, or several, as I did for a while, please try not to let it get to you. But do please also get some advice and wise support. Rising above it and not letting it affect you is very much easier said than done. Knowing that horrible things are being said about you publicly online is extremely unpleasant. But sadly it goes with the territory of being a leader these days. I got used to it, but I cannot pretend I found it easy to ignore.

One of my stalkers was a relative of a patient; we spent considerable time checking out the care the patient was receiving. We discovered that our staff had been putting up with face-to-face abuse over a number of years to an extent that was beyond unacceptable, which prompted us to act. I just wish we had known all this before; staff who work in mental health services can come to believe that abuse goes with the territory. It should not be so.

My most important advice of all is this. Please do not allow the fact that there are a tiny number of unpleasant people in the world to frighten you off using a medium that is open to all, and therefore more equal than anything else currently available. People will say things about you and the services you run online whether you are there or not. You might as well know what is being said so that you can decide whether to do anything about it.

Despite my experiences, I strongly disagree with those who say that public sector leaders shouldn't use social media because you are making yourself a target. That is a bit like saying that vulnerable people who go out alone are asking to be assaulted. I do know of leaders who have dipped their toe in the social media waters, come across a particularly nasty stalker, and left. I understand why, but I fear it is the wrong decision. I am not sure it is possible to be a public sector leader in today's world without social media.

Being an NHS Chief Executive

This blog from 2015 says things that I wish someone had told me when I was having a tough time on social media.

Please take care, Twitter can be cruel

I love Twitter. But it can be a cruel place. Personal attacks and even threats of death are not uncommon. Sue Perkins and Jack Monroe are the latest high-profile quitters following unrelated horridness – in Sue's case, she was attacked for being (wrongly) tipped as Jeremy Clarkson's replacement on Top Gear. Jack's was about supporting the Greens in the election. Death threats for this? There are no words.

I'm nowhere near their league, but I've had my share of online nastiness, and it continues. It can be overwhelming when you are under an onslaught from many directions. And unless you reply and risk even worse, other more measured folk won't know what's happening, because the vile stuff won't appear in their time line.

I am of the 'Whatever we wear and wherever we go, Yes means Yes and No means No' generation. I don't see why bullies should frighten us away from places that belong to us all. But I'm also concerned for my own wellbeing and that of others.

It is good that Twitter is cracking down on abuse – better late than never. Meanwhile, here are my tips for staying emotionally safe and still getting the best out of it:

1. *Be yourself but think really carefully about how much you share. Social media is still a relatively new medium. Some are already regretting earlier openness. I'm thinking particularly of people like me who experience mental illness from time to time. Talking with others who have similar experiences really helps, because with diseases of the mind, unchecked irrational thoughts about ourselves, can snowball and be really bad for us. But sharing also makes us vulnerable. Only a handful of people have accused me of psychological weakness,*

Please take care, Twitter can be cruel (cont.)

attention seeking or of using my depression as an excuse for past failings. Even fewer have defaced my image, called me vile names, and traduced my appearance, intelligence, morals, motivations and career. I have forgiven but I cannot forget their words. On a bad day, I imagine that others may feel the same way about me. On a really bad day, I may even agree with some of this shit. So please, take care.

2. Be wary of individual tweeters who follow few people themselves. They may say interesting stuff, but they are unlikely to be interested in an online conversation with you. Maybe you don't mind just reading their views? It's a good way to start, especially if you are shy. But most of us are on social media because we want to exchange thoughts, share experiences and ideas.

3. Don't just follow those you know you will agree with. It might feel cosy to be in a cocoon of like-minded folk, but it won't stimulate or enlighten. If it weren't for Twitter, we wouldn't know the odious extent of the views of, say, Katie Hopkins on people seeking asylum. What better spur to get the previously disaffected to vote than the thought of people like Hopkins (who always vote, by the way – they know their rights) getting more of a say than us? We need to know these things.

4. Take the plunge and join in conversations when you haven't got a view or are still making up your mind. Some people think that being open-minded, even undecided, is feeble or wishy-washy. I disagree. Just be sure that when you are in one of these discussions,

everyone is treated with politeness, including you. Be prepared to walk away if that doesn't happen.

5. *Join in with conversations that are happening at the time you are actually on Twitter. Prepare yourself so you don't feel too hurt if people whose views you admire don't respond. Just move on and chat to someone else. Don't assume people are being rude; they might be but that really isn't your problem. Easier said than done when you desperately want a reply, I know!*

6. *Try not to get involved in those angry ding-dongs where an increasing number of @names get added, until in the end there is no space to say anything. If you get copied in, these are best ignored, in my experience.*

7. *Don't be heavy-handed with the Block button. Some people collect blocks like trophies, and will proudly list you as a person who lacks empathy along with others you may prefer not to be associated with. And you won't know about this if you have blocked them. Save blocking for porn sites, annoying bots and people who are genuinely harassing you. And for the latter, do also report them. Twitter are rightly upping their game in dealing with online harassment. If you are being repeatedly harassed by someone, you may also need to check if they have other profiles. In my experience, these are relatively easy to spot. And do also report them to the police. They definitely do take action when serious threats are made.*

8. *My thoughts here are aimed mainly at people like me who are able to tweet as individuals. The freedom we enjoy compared to those in public positions cannot be*

Please take care, Twitter can be cruel (cont.)

underestimated. I've been in one of those jobs, and written about use of Twitter from that perspective elsewhere. It is great if such people can share something personal of themselves, but it is a big ask, given what can happen and the impacts. Which leads me to my final point.

9. *Don't rush to judgement of others. No-one knows what it's like to sit where they are sitting, other than themselves. Be kind, always. Never, ever make remarks like James May did recently about those who made death threats towards Sue Perkins. He only made a bad situation worse. If you can't be kind, walk politely but firmly away.I've blogged in the past about forgiveness. If you haven't seen it and are interested, you can find it on my blog site*

www.lisasaysthis.com/on-forgiveness-2

I'm still practising by the way.

Staff communications

What would I do about communications with staff if I were starting out today? Probably a short weekly vlog (video blog) rather than a weekly email/written blog. I'd want to make sure that everyone would be able to see the vlog, and have a really easy way of getting responses – because at least with an email, people can reply. And for those who don't have regular access to computers at work, such as housekeeping staff, I'd want to be sure it was shown somewhere convenient for them and was relevant to them. I'd ask people to join me and tell stories about the work that they do, or to make their own vlogs which I could refer to. And I would definitely still sign up to Twitter, because it is open and equal and anyway I could not live without it.

I would devote half day a week visiting services and teams and making sure I met frontline staff for Chatham House rules-type discussions, on what is good and what isn't working so well, to talk about our values and what motivates them to do the jobs they do, and what gets in the way. I would agree with them what they wanted me to feedback to their managers, so that I could share something that would be useful afterwards. I did more of this in my first and my final six months than the 12 years in between. I like to think it was valuable. And I wish that I had done it more.

As the wonderful Maya Angelou said:

'I have learned that people will forget what you said, people will forget what you did, but people will never forget how you made them feel.'

Being an NHS Chief Executive

Chapter 4

Abuse and whistleblowing

Introduction

I started writing this chapter in 2015, not long after the abuses of children and vulnerable young adults by the likes of Jimmy Savile, Rolf Harris, Cyril Smith and other high-profile figures started coming to light.

Back then, we knew there was more to come. And we also knew that convictions represented just a small part of the whole picture. The police admit to being overwhelmed. The Crown Prosecution Service has to conserve its resources for those cases where conviction is at least a possibility. And in some cases, public authorities appear to have colluded over many years to keep horrific allegations of abuse from the public eye for various misguided reasons.

Now it is 2018 and brave victims have started coming forward to allege and call out the gross and sexually predatory behaviour of Harvey Weinstein, Kevin Spacey and others. At last, we appear to be listening. We have seen members of the Cabinet and Her Majesty's Opposition resign over allegations of sexual misconduct while in public office.

The Independent Inquiry into Child Sexual Abuse has completed its preliminary work. It *'will investigate whether public bodies and other non-state institutions have taken seriously their duty of care to protect children from sexual abuse in England and Wales'*.

Since 2016, the inquiry has been led by Professor Alexis Jay OBE, a social worker. She is the fourth chair to have been appointed, the first two having been forced to resign over allegations that they were too close to people who might be later implicated in the inquiry, and the third for personal reasons. There have been several other high-profile resignations from the inquiry team. It appears to be both a thankless and perhaps impossible task.

We know that those who have been abused, but can be presented by defence lawyers to juries as unreliable witnesses, seldom get a fair time in court. And as happened for many years in Rotherham, and many other towns and cities, people who have been abused but are too fragile, inarticulate or badly damaged remain hidden from public view. Sadly, they may not be hidden from drug, alcohol and mental health services; domestic violence agencies; services that work with prostitutes; prisons, probation officers and social workers; bail and homeless hostels, and all the tireless and amazing charities that support those who have experienced abuse and grown not only to expect it but to believe that they deserve it, whose lives have been blighted by it, and who may never truly gain sufficient trust in others to speak up and receive the support they need.

I may sound angry. In fact, I feel part of the collective guilt of those in charge of public bodies. There is so much we could have known and done about these things. We seem obsessed with enquiries, but they produce the same findings: poor communication between the agencies; people in key positions missing vital warning signs; not believing vulnerable witnesses, even blaming them, time after time. Do we ever learn? I hope we do. But it has all been much too slow. And today, knowing all that we do, the tendency is to move ever more quickly from cursory sympathy for those affected, to pointing the finger of blame, fear and disgust at the alleged abuser, before they have even had a chance to hear the charges against them, never mind get a fair hearing. We need to be careful, because such public vilification can lead to awful consequences, such as the probable suicide of Welsh Assembly member Carl Sargeant.

And then we turn on those in positions of authority. Instead of responding with kindness to those affected, we demand to know why someone didn't do something at the time to stop the abuse, or missed all the warning signs that, with the benefit of hindsight, were so obvious and allowed the abuse to continue over decades.

In this chapter I am going to share my thoughts on all this, and look at how it links to the broader issue of whistleblowing.

A child of the 1960s

I was born in 1955. Being a child of the 1960s has had a profound effect on me, and those of my generation. The freedoms we experienced, compared with our parents who grew up with the privations and sorrows of World War 2 and whose own parents had lived through World War 1, were incomprehensible to that older generation.

But this freedom came at a cost. While most of our parents recoiled from the sexually provocative music of Jimi Hendrix and the Rolling Stones, my friends and I were intoxicated by it. We were glued to the BBC's *Top of the Pops*. We liked most of the DJs. But we were as one in our loathing of Jimmy Savile. With hindsight, how could anyone have missed what he was doing with his phallic cigar, bare chest and overt groping? He was revolting.

And yet none of us ever said anything to anyone about how disgusting he made us feel, apart from to each other, because nice girls didn't talk about such things. And we still wanted to get tickets for *Top of the Pops*; we knew we could dance better than most of the blank-faced girls cavorting in front of the cameras. It is now, of course, clear that we would have been unlikely to get tickets; we weren't vulnerable and living in an approved school or a mental hospital as many of those poor souls were. It makes me so sad to think of how those young people, my contemporaries, were used and abused. It could have been any one of us, had circumstances been different.

In the late 1960s and early 1970s, nice girls read magazines like *Jackie*. You learned how to use make-up to make it look 'natural', how to get into a car wearing a mini-skirt without showing your pants, and how to look sexy yet demure, like Twiggy or Jane Asher. Nice girls allowed boys to kiss them but you didn't make yourself 'cheap' by letting a boy 'have his way' - although you risked being called 'frigid' or a 'cock-teaser' if you refused. If a man whistled at you in the street or gave you a playful pinch of the bottom, you were expected to squeal sweetly. It was a compliment, after all. You were certainly not encouraged to complain. And if Uncle Ernie wanted you to sit on his lap and give him a cuddle, or worse, you were expected to put up with it.

Young people today find all this incredible, but it is how things were. And it is people, mainly men, from my generation who have until recently been in charge.

Whistleblowing

How does this link to whistleblowing?

As mentioned in Chapter 1, I started my nurse training in October 1973. The previous summer, aged just 18, I got a job as a nursing assistant at The Forest Hospital, in Horsham, West Sussex. It was a mile up the road from where my family lived, and I had passed it hundreds of times. I had occasionally wondered what went on behind those green railings; I knew it was some sort of hospital, and that Nissan huts had been added to the original Victorian workhouse building to accommodate injured Canadian servicemen during WW2. Now people lived there who couldn't look after themselves. But it wasn't considered polite to ask too many questions about places like that.

I suspect that nothing anyone could have said would have prepared me for what I found. The Forest Hospital had been incorporated into the NHS after the war, and had gradually become a centre for people who these days we would describe as having learning disabilities. Back then, it was officially known as a low-grade mental sub-normality unit, although the more acceptable term was a hospital for the mentally handicapped. And it was home to around 450 people, mostly adults but also some children.

There were two children's wards. The children on Highbeech 1 were considered to have enough mobility and communication to go to a special school. I was allocated to Highbeech 2, where the most profoundly disabled children lived. Many lay in their cots all day. The majority suffered from fits, and they were all doubly incontinent. A few could walk, although not well, and would fall and bang their heads if they were not constantly supervised. There were no special wheelchairs, just a few battered prams and pushchairs. When there was time, we would take some of the children outside. But that didn't happen very often.

We spent our days washing, changing, lifting, feeding and cuddling these children, and giving them their medicines. They had no words, but I gradually learned what some were trying to say with their squeaks and squawks and other little noises. I have thought about those children throughout my NHS career (see Chapter 2).

Forty years ago, most people with disabilities were shut away in institutions. Parents of such children would be told to hand them over to the authorities as babies, to forget they had ever had them and to get on with their lives, if possible by having another 'normal' child. This caused tremendous heartache for the parents and was very bad for the children. Luckily not everyone followed this advice. But many did, and so some of the children became adults who had no visitors.

There was a tendency for staff who worked in these large, shut-away institutions also to become institutionalised. Recruitment was difficult; despite attracting slightly higher pay rates than the more popular parts of the NHS, work with people with profound disabilities was low status and considered to be very difficult. Not many chose it as a career.

There was a steady flow of staff from the British colonies who came to the Forest Hospital and other such places to train as nurses in mental illness or mental handicap, sometimes because they had a vocation but mainly as entry to the UK. The majority of the staff, whether from the UK or overseas, lived in hospital accommodation, and their social lives revolved around the hospital. Relationships among staff were commonplace, and added to the spice of work.

I entered this world, and mostly I loved it. I wasn't surprised by the way that people with disabilities were locked away and denied the basic human right of living in their own homes with loving support so they could do the things that those without disabilities took for granted. We had no such expectations for people like that in those days. Enoch Powell, Minister of Health from 1960-1962, had made his ground-breaking 'water towers and chimneys' speech in 1961, and a few pioneers were writing papers and making plans, but the closure of the long stay hospitals and the move to the much-criticised although ultimately mainly successful Care in the Community didn't really get going until the 1980s. I have no excuse for not realising that the type of care we were giving was institutional abuse, but nor did anyone else. It was simply how things were.

Still, I was a bit shocked by some of the tales I heard, of staff who fed lighted cigarettes to a man who liked to eat them (everyone smoked on the wards in those days), of a woman who would take out her eye and put it in her food, until one day another patient snatched her bowl from her and ate it. And about a patient who had to be kept out of the ward kitchen because otherwise he would cram any food he could get his hands on into his mouth until he choked. And then one night a nurse stood by while he did so.

I have no idea if these lurid stories were true. I didn't see any of these things myself. The staff I worked with on Highbeech 2 were some of the loveliest people I have ever met. They were kind, knowledgeable, patient and extremely hardworking. They answered my incessant questions and taught me things I have always remembered, such as how to avoid retching when clearing up something not very nice, and how to make a safety helmet out of crepe bandages, bits of foam and Elastoplast. They would let me sit and cuddle the children and play with them even when there were other, less pleasant jobs to be done.

But I also heard about male nurses who were not allowed to work on the women or children's wards because they liked to do things to the patients that were too disgusting to repeat. Apparently, some of the female patients liked it when they did this, but others did not. The term sexual abuse had not been invented back then.

I believed these stories. They were fascinating as well as horrific. I can't remember whether I talked to anyone else first, but I do remember making a decision that I needed to do something about what I had heard. So off I went to see the person who I believed was in charge of the hospital. Memory is notoriously unreliable, and so I don't know if my recollection of a cosy, smoke-filled little office, a bottle of whisky on the filing cabinet, a manager with their feet up on the desk and a smelly old dog in a basket are true or figments of my imagination. I do know that I was asked what I wanted, and blurted it out, almost certainly in an excitable, breathless jumble. And I remember the next part very well.

Manager: *It's Nurse Rodrigues, isn't it?*

Me: *Yes*

Manager: *And I hear you are off to do your training soon?*

Me: *Yes*

Manager: *And where are you going to train?*

Me: *The Hospital for Sick Children, Great Ormond Street.*

Manager: *Well, Nurse Rodrigues, when you get to the Hospital for Sick Children, Great Ormond Street* (at this point I realise the interview isn't going well because the manager has started impersonating my squeaky, slightly posh teenage voice) *you will learn to keep your eyes open and your mouth shut. Now get out of my office.*

And that was my first, unsuccessful, attempt at whistleblowing. I've had better days.

Whistleblowing has been in the news since the scandals I mentioned earlier. It shouldn't need to happen, in the NHS or in any organisation. Staff should get good supervision, and be able to raise any concerns they have with a person they trust who is wise, well-informed, and empowered to help. And where there is a suggestion that someone has been or might be hurt, such concerns should be looked into carefully and speedily, and dealt with effectively and with compassion.

But real life isn't like that. Only some managers are good at this part of their jobs, or get sufficient training, experience and help to improve how they respond to staff who raise concerns. Not all organisations have policies that are fit for purpose. And even if they have, they may not be used as they were intended. Worse, the policies may be used as excuses not to act.

It is important to remember that there are at least two sides to every story. Investigations can lead to damned-if-you-do-and-damned-if-you-don't outcomes, and not all senior managers are brave enough or supported enough to make the right call - or what they hope will turn out to be the least bad call.

My belief is that most instances of abuse and neglect in the NHS are caused by lack of visible, effective leadership in clinical settings, allowing casual neglect and abusive behaviour to move from the exception to the norm. Lack of good local leaders are symptoms of a wider organisational malaise, of cutting corners, or hitting a target but missing the point of why it was set.

Boards and commissioners can become focussed on balancing the books and achieving organisational goals to the detriment of their main purpose, and not be alert to the impact of their decisions on patients. This is what appears to have happened at Mid Staffordshire Hospitals and at Winterbourne View[3]

Reliable witnesses

Not all whistle-blowers turn out to be reliable witnesses. There have been a small number of high profile, wrongful arrests where people who in all probability haven't been abused jumped on the bandwagon because there is fame, of sorts, and compensation to be had. Paul Gambaccini has written about his own experiences of wrongful arrest, and the negative media coverage that arose from the police tipping off the press even before charges had been brought. I know two talented, honourable people whose careers were ended and lives badly affected by false allegations from vulnerable people who thought they could make some money via a poorly-run compensation scheme.

And I recall one specific case, when I was a nurse director. I received a long letter alleging serious abuse and neglect of vulnerable patients.[4] The letter contained mainly opinions and value judgements, but nonetheless I and my executive colleagues took the allegations seriously and agreed they must be investigated. I met the member of staff who had written the letter. This person seemed plausible; they had just returned from an extended period of sick leave for stress during which they described having an

---

[3] The Mid Staffordshire Enquiry reported in 2013
www.gov.uk/government/publications/report-of-the-mid-staffordshire-nhs-foundation-trust-public-inquiry and the Winterbourne View Review in the same year
https://www.gov.uk/government/publications/winterbourne-view-hospital-department-of-health-review-and-response Both are essential reading for NHS chief executives, because they show what can happen if you lose sight of your main purpose.

[4] Fortunately, it was signed. Unsigned letters cannot be investigated and must simply be filed. But they may still give you sleepless nights, which is why they are extremely unhelpful.

epiphany and deciding they could no longer ignore the things they alleged.

An executive colleague and I instigated an investigation. We interviewed a considerable number of staff, patients and families, and pored over sets of records. We uncovered one or two fairly toxic relationships within the service, including some counter allegations about the competence and motivation of the member of staff who had written the letter, but no signs of the alleged abuse and, indeed, some very good examples of care. We eventually concluded that, while we didn't actually disbelieve the member of staff, we could find no evidence of abuse or neglect.

What to do? The member of staff, who I had placed on special leave so that the investigation could be carried out, said they wanted to return to the service. But the relationship between them and their manager, who was relatively inexperienced, and with their other colleagues who had been accused, had broken down irretrievably. I didn't attempt mediation because the member of staff was still adamant that their colleagues were guilty and were now also covering it up.

Perhaps I should have, because what happened next wasn't great either. I worked hard to find a suitable alternative role. The placement lasted less than a week. The member of staff went off sick again and made a series of new allegations. Eventually they left in difficult circumstances. I don't regret the original investigation, because the allegations might all have been true. But I suspect the impact on the staff about whom the allegations were made was significant, and that the whole thing affected them and their patients. And I doubt we supported them well enough either during the investigation or afterwards, for which I am truly sorry.

Shining a light into dark corners

Celebrity whistle-blowers are a recent phenomenon. These are members of staff, patients or bereaved families who, having failed to be listened to via the more traditional means, have turned to the media, especially social media, to be heard. Some have lost their livelihoods and their homes and had their health badly affected over their fight for justice. They are usually highly principled, driven people who are not prepared to be ignored or fobbed off, and believe that their case is an example from which lessons can be learned and changes made. I think we should be grateful to them. They shine a light into dark corners, and help us remember what we are here for. In straitened times for health and care services, this is increasingly valuable.

In any group, there is the occasional bad apple, someone who jumps on the bandwagon for their own purposes or who misrepresents the facts. But these are rare. I have come to know quite a few whistle-blowers via social media, and made some good friends. I truly believe we are on the same side.

My advice to wannabe chief executives is to keep an open mind and an open door. People you think are completely trustworthy may be hiding a nasty secret. But equally, ask the best of people at the outset and the majority will rise to the occasion. And listen, really hard, because the truth will be out there somewhere.

Values

Finally, and this is really important, we can all become blind to the foibles of someone who, if we met them afresh, we would realise straightaway has undesirable tendencies. I don't mean people who are eccentric, by the way – every organisation needs those. They are pearls who should be nurtured, because they are often original thinkers who tend not to toe the party line. If you listen carefully, they will help you to spot the charlatans.

However, I have learned to my cost that it is not really possible for someone to be a good clinician or manager if they can't get on with their peers. Those who behave in a bullying manner towards more junior staff, but when you raise it with them claim they are being bullied themselves, are more often than not in need of some focussed attention. It is more than likely that the same poor behaviour will occur with patients or affect patients in some other way.

I have in the past been guilty of putting up with poor behaviour from some clinicians AND from the occasional manager which, with hindsight, was damaging to morale and reputation. In my latter years, I became more confident at tackling this. We started to do a lot more work on values, commitments and behaviours, discovering it is good to be explicit about these things. We all have off days, of course, but being welcoming, friendly, helpful, listening carefully to others, sticking with the agreed task and showing hope are essential if you work in the caring professions.

And that includes chief executives.

Chapter 5

Sex, work and the abuse of power

Introduction

You may be surprised that the word 'sex' appears in the chapter title of a book like this.

Actually, it isn't so much about sex but rather about what sexual attraction means in a work context. I have thought about this quite a lot. I hope it will help you and others.

It used to be said that we each think about sex approximately once every seven seconds. Then it was clarified that the study had only included men and was in any case considerably flawed.

The truth, according to Tom Stafford, writing on the BBC Futures website[5], is that we don't really know how often people think about sex, but that it occurs fairly frequently, including throughout the working day.

What we each do in the privacy of our own relationships and in our private lives is absolutely none of anyone else's business. Or it shouldn't be, as long as there is equality between the protagonists. I have issues with the sort of sex that is a metaphor for power, which has been a recurring theme throughout my working life and perhaps yours. In mental health services, power is an emotive, misunderstood and often misused concept.

This short chapter is divided into three sections: sex between work colleagues, sex between patients, and sex with patients. I have included some examples, anonymised for reasons that will be

---

[5] http://www.bbc.com/future/story/20140617-how-often-do-men-think-about-sex

obvious when you read them. Some details have been changed to protect vulnerable people. But they are all based on true cases.

Sex between colleagues

Apparently, the most common place to meet your future life partner is at work. Not a surprise, considering how much time we all spend at work. So not a problem. Hopefully...

In all probability, you have been part of a team in which a couple of other team members were having a clandestine 'thing'. They may have been in the early stages of a relationship that might grow into something more long-term and didn't want to jeopardise it with the intrusion of prurient or otherwise unhelpful interest from others. Or perhaps it was a dalliance that one or other felt had no future. Maybe one or both of them were in another supposedly permanent relationship and were, to put it politely, playing away from home. Each of these scenarios has the potential to be uncomfortable for all concerned.

When you are the boss and something like this is happening within your team, you need to decide whether it is affecting team dynamics and performance, and what, if anything, to do about it. You may decide for the time being to do nothing. But the one thing you mustn't do is simply ignore it. You will have to make a conscious decision whether to act or leave well alone. If you act, you may have to face some socially awkward conversations. But if you don't, and morale and performance suffer, or there are perceived or actual conflicts of interest, you will almost certainly come to regret not having had those conversations.

Later on, after very careful consideration, you may decide that in order to address the potential for conflicts of interest such relationships create, you need to make changes to reporting arrangements, even to restructure. To take it to a more extreme level, you may even conclude that one of the parties must move jobs or even leave. When you are making such decisions, I would just say this: please do all that you can to make sure you don't disadvantage the more junior person in the relationship. This is harder than it sounds. If the relationship is heterosexual, it is more than likely that the woman will be the more junior member of staff. You will have legal, but more importantly moral, obligations to consider.

There are no easy answers. Be compassionate, be fair, be consistent and try to avoid making value judgements. But most of all, remember that pretending you don't know is the coward's response .

Now, supposing it is you, the chief executive, who is causing a bit of gossip, even consternation, because you are 'seeing' a member of staff? This is not uncommon. I have known CEs who have had relationships at work with people who directly report to them, who report to people who report to them, or who report to people who report to people etc.

Some of these CEs have been free to do this, in the sense that they were unencumbered by another relationship. But the other person might not have been free. I have also known CEs who were in supposedly permanent relationships and yet seemed incapable of keeping their metaphorical trousers up when someone attractive appeared on the scene. I'm not being sexist here; women do also wear trousers to work these days.

I will simply say this. As the CE of any organisation, however large or small, you are everyone's ultimate boss. The power you wield is greater than that of anyone else. However easy-going, approachable, caring and adorable you may think you are, and whatever your gender or sexuality, you represent something to the people who work for you that means that any personal relationship will invariably be unequal.

Because you can promote them, pay them more money, and apply your patronage and influence to improve their working conditions and opportunities in any number of other ways. You can also fire them. And because of this, the power you hold is, of itself, seductive. In other words, they may not really fancy you, but rather, they are attracted, even enthralled, by the position of power that you hold. I'm sorry if that comes as a surprise. But it is a fact you will have to get used to. To abuse that power is, in my view, pretty close to unforgiveable.

So please, please think very carefully before doing it.

The *Daily Mail* is not known for its love of public sector managers. It is also not a newspaper I would normally choose to read. But it does have one great use, which I call the *Daily Mail* test. There will be many times in your chief executive life that you will be able to use my *Daily Mail* test. This is one of those times. How would you feel if what you are thinking about doing with this apparently irresistible other person were to appear as a story on the front page of the *Daily Mail*? For these reasons, my advice is as follows: try with all your considerable willpower not, under any circumstances, to consider a relationship with a member of your staff. In fact, go as far as possible out of your way to avoid such a thing.

And if you do fall in love with someone at work, despite doing everything you possibly can to avoid it, check your feelings for them and also how they feel about you by giving up the job. Then you can both see for real how the relationship fares.

Finally, to various unnamed yet notorious NHS leaders who invite young, ambitious yet vulnerable NHS staff members for tea/a drink/a meal and via that to the NHS version of the casting couch, I simply say this: you know who you are.

And you are, in my opinion, despicable.

Sex between patients

I remember the comments of an experienced female psychiatrist, when one of her (male) colleagues was waxing lyrical on how the introduction of single bedrooms in psychiatric hospitals was playing havoc with our costs. Put simply, we needed more nursing staff on duty per shift because there were many more places for patients to be able to hide unobserved and then to hurt themselves.

I can't remember her exact words, but she remarked, somewhat laconically, that at least she could now admit her female patients without fear of them getting raped. The colleague poo-pooed her. But I have never forgotten this. And I know from talking to female and to male patients that rape and sexual assault by other patients, while less common than they used to be, remain a hazard in most mental hospital settings and in other NHS settings where vulnerable people receive care. Much importance is placed these days on gender separation. But while it can help, it is not in any way a panacea for sexual safety. The only way to achieve that is by constant vigilance and expert, compassionate clinical care, including there being enough trained and experienced staff to make such care a reality.

Unfortunately, some mental illnesses and some treatments for mental illnesses decrease inhibitions and/or increase libido. And people who are admitted to mental hospitals are invariably vulnerable. I recall an occasion when we had invited a TV film-crew in to see some improvements we had made at one of our hospitals. At the sight of the cameras, one very unwell lady immediately started disrobing, until she was kindly and skilfully supported to move somewhere more private by one of the nurses. Something similar happened at another time and place during a Christmas carol concert; the Salvation Army choir were very open-minded about the naked man who emerged from under a pile of coats in a state of arousal. Again, the situation was handled with great compassion and skill by the nurses.

It has always troubled me when relationships develop between patients who are unwell. I have looked into various complaints made by individuals and families after such occurrences, and it seems both extraordinary but also understandable that staff feel unable to intervene sufficiently to keep vulnerable people safe. This is probably because, when staff do try to act to protect a vulnerable person, they can receive an extremely strong response and be subject to complaints from the people concerned. So I do know how difficult this is.

This isn't something that only happens in mental hospitals. I recall a young orthopaedic patient somehow becoming pregnant despite being in an open hospital ward with both legs in traction. Some people thought it was amusing. All I could think was that she was only eighteen.The trouble with all the great work done in recent years to protect vulnerable adults is that, in the circumstances I describe, there are often two vulnerable people. And while a relationship might be a good thing for one of the people concerned, it may be far less so for the othe one.

As a leader, you can make sure such matters are carefully discussed in team meetings, that staff understand their responsibilities to vulnerable people, and that there are wise psychologists available to help work through how to tackle such matters with sensitivity and an eye to considering the needs of the most vulnerable person concerned.

I am sorry that there are no easy answers here.

Sex between staff and patients

It may seem incredible to those reading this now, but when I started my nurse training in 1973, there were no rules to make it clear that relationships between staff and patients were taboo. I recall working with a nurse who was married to someone who had been her patient in intensive care. This person had an ongoing serious health condition, and the couple were now having some relationship issues. At the time, Mills and Boon published romantic novels about nurses marrying glamorous young patients, usually soldiers who had lost a leg or become paralysed in war. And there have been a number of real-life famous men with disabilities who have married their nurses.

But such relationships are almost inevitably problematic because, again, the power balance is unequal. I know this because of my own reactions to people who have looked after me when I have been vulnerable. I apparently expressed undying love for the dentist after he removed a tooth using intravenous Valium (never done these days for safety reasons); I had to be carried from the surgery, weeping, by my husband. After giving birth to our daughter, I became obsessed with the midwife who had delivered me, and fantasised about her calling round to tell me how beautiful my baby was and how well I had done. And when I had my last major depression, I became more than a little fixated on those who looked after me.

The majority of those who choose to work with vulnerable people do so because they are compassionate and caring and believe they can make a difference. But as with any group, there is a normal distribution curve. At one end of the graph, people are motivated entirely by altruism and kindness, and would never abuse their position under any circumstances. Most of us fall somewhere in the middle of the curve. We would not abuse our positions, but we are there not entirely for altruistic motives. We have a need to be needed, which we manage with varying degrees of awareness and skill. And at the opposite end of the curve are people who choose to be there for nefarious purposes and will create opportunities to abuse their power and do terrible things to vulnerable people.

Chapter Four of this book is on abuse and whistleblowing. It includes a description of the changes in attitudes that have occurred during my working life. It is good that vulnerable people, including children, are now coming forward to say what has happened to them, using words that we can all understand. They are no longer automatically disbelieved or even blamed for the terrible things that have happened to them.

The fact remains, however, that abuse is often a significant part of what leads to mental illness in the first place. These changes are still relatively recent, and the burden of proof remains with the person who has been abused.

A brief story from the mid-1990s

I was Director of Nursing and on call. The phone rang at about 1 am. A female patient on one of the acute mental wards had accused a male nurse of sexually assaulting her. The police had been called but did not feel they could act, given that she was in hospital and her doctor had apparently refused them permission to interview her.

I agreed with the nurse in charge to send the nurse who had been accused home, provide cover and investigate the following morning. When I spoke to senior colleagues the next day, they were disparaging about the veracity of the claim. They also questioned my right to investigate.

I ploughed on, and can remember meeting the patient. She was very poorly and either wouldn't or couldn't speak to me. I talked to the staff who had been present, and the nurse himself, and it was all somewhat inconclusive. I agreed that the nurse could return to work.

When I looked at the patient's notes (being a nurse myself made this possible) what became clear was that she had a long history of describing being assaulted which seemed to stem from sexual abuse as a teenager . And yet her care took no account of this. And her doctor, who was furious with me for what he described as my over-reaction, told me that he had threatened to section her if she made any more such, in his words, allegations.

I will never know whether she had been assaulted on that particular occasion. But I do know that the care she received was not sensitive to her traumatic history.

> *And in later years, I learned just how important it is to listen to people who have been abused, and how such abuse has a severe impact on future wellbeing, especially when it is dismissed, as hers was.*
>
> *Just imagine being her, or someone like her, and how frightening it must be not to be believed. And yet we hear stories like this all the time. There is still much to be done.*

One of the most memorable things that I learned as a leader is that whatever safeguards you put in place, people will occasionally do things that are more terrible than you could ever possibly imagine. When colleagues have suspicions about those who groom vulnerable patients, we can encourage them to blow the whistle and share their concerns, and not to worry if these prove to be unfounded. But it is sometimes people who seem extremely plausible, kind and caring that perpetrate the worst abuses.

Politicians, regulators and others who sit in judgement on those of us who only find out about such awful behaviour after the event sometimes expect us to have had the benefit of foresight. But we cannot and never will. We can produce as many policies and safeguards as it is possible to create. They will sometimes help. But they will also get in the way of giving care to people because they are time-consuming and unwieldy - such as a no-touch policy which sounds sensible but can feel unnatural and inhumane when put into practice. And we will never be able to stop every person who is determined to abuse their power with those who are vulnerable.

The Jimmy Savile case and others like it have given voice to a small but vocal group of conspiracy theorists. They would have vulnerable people believe that everyone who works in health or social care is either an abuser or complicit in the abuse by others. I find this troubling but also a sad fact of life. Social media means that we hear more from such people than we used to.

The good news is that we are slowly getting better at talking about sexual abuse, and what constitutes it. Part of the problem in the past was that 'nice' people avoided discussing it, and if it came up in conversation they would become uncomfortable and change the subject. This meant that those who experienced it often felt too ashamed to say that it had happened to them.

There is a growing and persuasive body of thought that sees abuse as a main causative factor in mental illness, but it is not quite as simple as abuse = breakdown.

Some people seem to have an innately stronger emotional resilience than others, which seems to grow from having someone important, such as (but not always) a mother, who shows them unconditional love and affection in their early years. This is what humanistic psychologist Carl Rogers calls Unconditional Positive Regard[6]. The work by Professor Avi Sagi-Schwartz, writing in *The Atlantic* magazine on the resilience of Holocaust survivor draws further on this theory[7]. An important aspect is how early the abuse occurred, and whether there has been a primary care giver who stepped in to protect the person, failed to protect them but would have done so had they known, or whether they colluded with or even carried out the abuse.

During my time at Sussex Partnership, we started a programme of talking about sexual abuse which we called The Big Conversation. It made people uncomfortable at first, but it also unlocked some important discussions in teams. I don't think we did nearly enough of it, but it was a good beginning.

---

[6] www.bapca.org.uk/about/carl-rogers
[7] www.theatlantic.com/international/archive/2013/09/male-holocaust-survivors-lived-longer-than-those-who-escaped-europe/279462/

If you are taking on a job where people are vulnerable, which in my view means the whole of the NHS, or indeed any work that involves giving personal care to people, I suggest you work out how best to do the same. Because talking helps people, both patients and staff, find the words to say the things that are troubling them the most.

And if that makes even just one vulnerable person safer, it will have been worth it.

Being an NHS Chief Executive

Chapter 6

The stigma and discrimination of mental illness: what this means and how it manifests itself

To anyone who says that we have cracked the stigma of mental illness, because a few of us have 'come out' about experiencing various forms of it, and Time to Change has been able to show a small but measurable shift in attitudes since 2007, I would say this: yes, there has been some change, but we have only just scratched the surface.

Stigma surrounding those who experience mental illness is still present and unfair discrimination towards such people and the services that should be there to support them is stigma's ugly sister. This chapter is my attempt to bring some of this further into the open.

My early efforts to tackle stigma

When I first became a mental health trust chief executive at the end of 2001, I decided to make tackling stigma one of my top priorities. This appeared in our strategy and plans from 2002 onwards and was still an essential part of the plan for 2014/15, the year I left. I began by trying to talk to colleagues in other parts of the NHS about the stigma of mental illness, with limited success. To start with, they were pretty unreceptive.

I remember giving a presentation to colleagues in Kent, Surrey and Sussex about the prevalence of self-harm, substance misuse and alcohol related harm among people presenting in accident and emergency departments, and of dementia among patients in acute hospitals who had been admitted for other reasons. I recall this being rather less than warmly received. They challenged the facts presented and appeared to have no concerns about stigma.

They were wrong, but I obviously wasn't very good at persuading them - yet. I also recall, in 2003, that one of these same acute trust chief executive called me away from a meeting to tell me in no uncertain terms that his emergency department had got what he described as 'one of yours' in it, and that I needed to do something urgently because this person was causing havoc and smashing the place up. It turned out that the patient was a person with a learning disability who had broken his arm some days earlier. He had been brought back to hospital by ambulance in a state of extreme distress. According to my colleague, he was roaring at the top of his voice and hitting out with his plaster cast at the doctors and nurses who tried to calm him down. There was considerable damage to the department. When one of our senior doctors arrived to see him, the problem was immediately obvious: the poor man's hand was slowly turning black because the plaster cast had been applied too tightly. It was removed and he immediately stopped shouting. It still shocks me that it took a psychiatrist to see this. All anyone else could see was a person with a learning disability, rather than a man in acute pain.

At around the same time, I remember Sir Nigel (now Lord) Crisp, then NHS chief executive and Permanent Secretary at the Department of Health, referring kindly but somewhat disparagingly to what he called 'the mental health lobby'. Sadly, I knew just what he meant. At any large scale event involving senior NHS leaders, as soon as questions were invited from the floor, a hand would shoot up and a not very well-formulated question along the lines of 'and what about mental health services?' would be posed.

Sir Nigel's point, which I agreed with, was that we needed to make our case for increased investment and better information, and develop a shared understanding of why mental health mattered across the whole of the NHS, rather than just to those who worked in it. Some of the other, more experienced mental health trust chief executives, including Stuart Bell, then at South London and Maudsley NHS Trust, Stephen Firn at Oxleas, and Erville Millar at Camden and Islington, shared my concerns. They listened to my ramblings and helped by allocating time at our national mental health collaboration, a group which we steered to become incorporated into the NHS Confederation as the Mental Health Network. Together, we devised a project which we called Mainstreaming Mental Health. One of our key arguments was that, without the hard-edged targets applied to other parts of the NHS, our services were at a continuous disadvantage.

Together we made a good case, and in 2005 received a promise from Sir Nigel that work would begin on developing a national contract currency for mental health services, despite many people believing this should be left in the Too Difficult box. From 2006 – 2010, colleagues in the North West, working with others at the centre of the NHS, devised their 21-cluster model, which came extremely close to being implemented nationally.

But it never made it. The fact is that, as I finish writing this book in 2018, there remains no contract currency for mental health services. Mental health services are still commissioned using myriad methods that do not compare like with like.

Services across the country not only remain disparately commissioned. They are also disparately reported on and funded. This leads to mental health care being literally a postcode lottery. Parity of esteem for mental health services, a term that has been in use for a long time but which was adopted with much trumpeting by the government in 2010 and is supposedly still policy today, remains no more than a vague aspiration.

The National Service Framework for Mental Health

Mental health trust leaders and staff who have been around as long as I was look back on the good old days of the National Service Framework for Mental Health, devised by the brilliant Professor Louis Appleby CBE, with some wistfulness.

Louis was at the time National Clinical Director for Mental Health, also known as the Mental Health Czar, from 2000 – 2010. I cannot imagine anyone less like a czar. Louis went on to be the national Clinical Director for Mental Health in Criminal Justice, and a Non-Executive Director at the Care Quality Commission. He continues to practise psychiatry and to lead the National Confidential Enquiry into Suicides and Homicides via his department at the University of Manchester. Louis is unassuming, but also laser-sharp in his brilliance. He is an all-time hero to mental health services and patients.

Back in the early 2000s, the NHS was, in relative terms compared with today, awash with money. In its second term, the Labour government had delivered on its promise of implementing the findings of the Wanless report. Most trusts saw annual investments over the next few years in excess of 3 per cent *above* the rate of inflation.

Compare that to below inflation level 'uplifts', flat cash, or in many cases significant reductions net of inflation that we hear about today. I and millions of others should be forever grateful to Louis for his vision in describing a service based on seven standards. These included better access in primary care, 24-hour crisis response, better care for people with psychosis including early intervention via specialist teams, and more assertive treatment, also via specialist teams. And perhaps most radically, it included a national approach to reducing the occurrence of suicide. Louis also gave us some hard measures for investment in new services, and ensured these were monitored via the ten powerful Strategic Health Authorities, who held PCT commissioners to account for their investment decisions.

Louis' legacy to people who work in mental health services, and those of us who from time to time need to use them, are a set of standards that still hold true today and against which we can still benchmark many aspects of care. They may need some modification to fit with our new, more digital and plural age, but they remain peerless in their vision and utility.

No Health Without Mental Health?

Many of the national reporting requirements that were so carefully designed by Louis and the excellent team that worked with him were unpicked following the reorganisation of the NHS under the coalition government in 2010.

Wise people from all political parties are coming to the realisation that the 2010 reorganisation will eventually come to be regarded in historical terms as the most disruptive and least productive NHS reorganisation ever.

The Guardian, February 2015:

The coalition's shake-up of the NHS was misguided, deepened the growing problems facing A&E units and left it weaker, structurally 'incomprehensible' and less able to improve care for patients, according to leading health think tank The Kings Fund.

For me, the worst aspect of the reforms, apart from the total chaos they caused for several years during the very time the NHS needed to pull together and concentrate on managing more demand with less money, has been to say one thing about mental health but at the same time to do precisely the opposite.

With the majority of national reporting on mental health investment having been lost through the demise of the Strategic Health Authorities, trusts continued to gather information on investment. This made it possible for investigative journalists such as Andy McNicholl of *Community Care*, Michael Buchanan of the BBC and Shaun Lintern of *Health Service Journal* to reveal that, while saying loudly and clearly that there was to be No Health Without Mental Health (the name of the mental health strategy launched by the coalition government early in its life in February 2011), the reality turned out to be the opposite.

By 2014, the levels of investment in mental health services had dropped to a ten-year low as a proportion of all NHS spend, from 13 per cent to 12 per cent. By 2017, it was 11 per cent. And given that mental health is acknowledged to be at least 25 per cent of the disease burden of the whole NHS, markedly more if you believe that there really is no health without mental health, this is a national disgrace.

Such unfair treatment is only possible **because of** the continued stigma and discrimination against mental illness and the services that are designed to support people who experience it. Imagine the outcry if, for example, the people responsible for commissioning cancer services were to say to those who provide them that they would be cutting their funding because they need to make savings, but not to worry because they will be investing a small proportion of the savings back into preventative or primary care services? We would see people marching on the streets.

The fact that there has been no national outcry, despite these cuts in mental health services being publically known, is evidence that we have a great deal more to do.

The stigma within the NHS

I started this chapter with a few words about my early efforts to get colleagues across the NHS and in the South East to embrace mental health and its relevance to the whole sector. We have come a long way since those days.

But when times get tough, people revert to behaviours they learned when they were less well-informed. One of my deepest regrets is that, in all my years as a chief executive, and with all the influence I had, I never truly managed to get our commissioners and partners to see improving mental health as our collective responsibility. They were always happy to accept the contributions of mental health and related services to achieving what were seen as real priorities, such as the four-hour target in A&E. But they were not so interested in helping the services I led to be the best they could be, clearly linked to receiving a fair share of the resources.

There seems to be an unwritten rule across most of the NHS: collective efforts and working together mean doing whatever it takes to achieve the targets of others but never mention the importance or challenge of achieving those of your own. That is, unless you run an acute trust.

I admit that I broke that rule from time to time, but only when I had agreed with my team and board that we had exhausted all other avenues.

Acute trusts regularly called for arbitration over their annual contracts. I generally viewed the need to go to arbitration as a sign of collective failure, although some judge it as quite a sport. In 13 years I only did so once, early in 2013, when we were due to lose £5 million the following year for something that was very clearly not our responsibility. It was the right thing to do but it still felt extremely uncomfortable, and I did so only after lengthy discussion with our board. We prepared our case carefully and were successful in arbitration, in fact to the tune of £7.4 million in our favour. But I don't think the commissioners ever really forgave me. In fact, I know they did not.

Another unwritten rule was that those in senior positions like mine who were not leading acute services should never publically admit to evidence of growth in demand, even when it was staring us in the face. Each year we would submit the evidence of such growth to our commissioners, and they would spend the next 11 months doing everything possible to undermine our figures. This was wearisome for all concerned, and would not have been necessary had we been on the sort of cost and volume or cost per case contract that we had been promised for so many years.

Also, each year, around November, we would be called at very short notice to urgent meetings to address the winter emergency problems facing acute trust providers. Until 2012 this was with the

SHA and NHS Executive, latterly with NHS England once they came into existence. My experience of such meetings was that they could be extremely intimidating. We would all be required to pledge support to deliver the A&E target, and many plans would be produced.

In contrast, meetings were only ever called to talk about my trust's services when we were being criticised for an incident or a report that was less than favourable.

I recall a public meeting in 2014 with a local authority in an area where we had recently taken on a contract to provide Children and Young People's Mental Health Services. The level of demand was approaching double what we had been told, and there were lengthy waiting lists that had been hidden at the time when we were finalising the contract negotiations. We had also inherited a demoralised workforce with a less than ideal skill mix and much higher rates of vacancy in key clinical positions than we had been informed.

Just over a year into a five-year contract, we were beginning to meet the revised targets that had been negotiated with some considerable difficulty. In a public meeting that was recorded on a webcam and which I was still able to watch two years later, a very pleasant locally elected member told me that she and other elected members truly believed that when we won the contract, we had been set up to fail.

This sort of thing is not in any way peculiar to the South East. Since retiring, I can be more vocal. I have noticed that some of the people who should be making the most impact about improvement seem to be closely wedded to maintaining the status quo. Here is a version of something I wrote the year after I retired about the recently published NHS Five Year Forward View[8]

---

[8] www.england.nhs.uk/wp-content/uploads/2014/10/5yfv-web.pdf.

If I ruled the world….

In a previous life, I ran a mental health trust for 13 years. It was really hard, but it brought some influence to bear on something that matters very much, that is the experiences of one in four people, who, like me, are sometimes mentally ill.

In 2010, as chair of the Mental Health Network, I shared a platform with Health Minister Paul Burstow MP, Paul Jenkins, then chief executive of Rethink, Sarah Brennan of Young Minds and others at the launch of the coalition government's mental health strategy No Health Without Mental Health.

And in 2013, I met Norman Lamb (who took over the ministerial role in 2012) and a few other senior colleagues to discuss why it was that the strategy hadn't worked, in our opinion. The shocking evidence of widespread disinvestment in mental health services was by then becoming clearer, rigorously uncovered by investigative journalists Shaun Lintern (HSJ), Andy McNicholl (Community Care) and Michael Buchanan (BBC). Heroes in my opinion.

In times of plenty, mental health services have received at least a small share of extra available resources. Professor Louis Appleby's excellent National Service Framework was delivered from 1999-2009 through increased investment in crisis services, early intervention and assertive outreach teams. And it was strictly monitored. Commissioners and/or trusts who thought they knew better than the best evidence of what underpinned compassionate, effective care for people with serious mental illness were found out and given no option but to improve. The architecture that supported this monitoring has since been

If I ruled the world....(cont.)

dismantled. We are left with regulation, inspection, adverse incident reporting and stories in the media.

The pressure by local commissioners on providers to swallow the current disinvestment medicine is considerable. Mental health leaders who make a fuss are viewed as lacking loyalty to their local health system. Were the same cuts made to cancer or heart services, there would be national uproar.

This tells us something, which is that stigma surrounding the mentally ill is alive and kicking within the NHS.

A true story: the other day, I mentioned the previous day's Dispatches programme entitled Kids in Crisis to someone senior from NHS England. I could tell they were irritated to be reminded that very sick children are currently languishing in police cells or being shipped hundreds of miles around the country while desperate clinicians spend hours trying to find a bed. This person actually said that parents are prepared to travel all over the world looking for the best treatment for conditions such as cancer. So why should CAMHS be different? When I reminded them that this wasn't about highly specialist care, just access to care anywhere, they blamed the failure on local services and moved on from talking to me to share their insights with someone else.

So, we have denial about the impact of disinvestment, as well stigma. And I realise that in my new freelance world, I have a different sort of influence.

Regarding the NHS Five Year Forward View (5YFV) here's my six-point plan for making mental health more mainstream. With measurements. Because if you don't measure, you can't manage.

1. Suicide prevention

Make suicide prevention the business of every citizen of the UK. Stop blaming mental health trusts and their staff for failing to keep people alive. The responsibility is much broader than that. Locate suicide reduction planning with Health and Wellbeing boards. Make it their number one priority, with proper support as well as sanctions for lack of progress.

2. Mental health within the NHS

Expect every provider and commissioner to make the care of people who happen to experience mental illness their explicit business. Start with primary care. Require every NHS employee, including reception staff and everyone who works in a commissioning organisation, to do a minimum half-day training, with an annual update, delivered by experts by experience. Report on compliance via the annual NHS staff survey.

3. Integration

Require local systems to produce integrated commissioning plans for all primary and secondary services. Particularly crisis care; dementia; all major physical conditions such as heart disease, strokes, obesity, diabetes and cancer; neurological conditions such as multiple sclerosis (MS) and motor neurone disease (MND); and musculoskeletal conditions including chronic pain. Draw on the Rapid Assessment Interface and Discharge (RAID) model for measurement. Allow organisational form to flower according to local need. But also require

If I ruled the world....(cont.)

investment in integrated services through an annual reduction in organisational overheads, and increased investment in the third sector.

4. Public health

Reduce premature death rates of up to 25 years in people with serious mental illnesses by making mental health promotion core business for primary care and secondary health providers in the statutory and non-statutory sectors. Target supportive, evidence-based obesity reduction, smoking cessation, substance misuse, harm reduction and exercise programmes for people with diagnoses such as schizophrenia, bipolar disorder, post-traumatic stress disorder (PTSD) and personality disorder. Set ambitious targets over the next 25 years and monitor hard against them to help turn around the life chances of some of the most marginalised people in society.

5. Making the business case

It is up to the NHS to articulate and prove the business case for a change of approach in welfare for people with long term conditions such as serious mental illnesses. Commission the best brains, such as Professor Martin Knapp at the London School of Economics to put the evidence together. It is considerably more costly as well as more cruel to condemn people who experience mental illness to poor, insecure housing and limited, insecure income, and for them to appear frequently and often pointlessly within criminal justice services.

But these costs do not occur in one place. Creating exciting opportunities for engagement and volunteering (such as the

Dragon Café (www.dragoncafe.co.uk) can help people move from being recipients to full participants. Placing employment specialists within mental health teams and incentivising pathways into work (see Centre for Mental Health on Employment: the economic case www.centreformentalhealth.org.uk/employment-the-economic-case) are also proven to be highly successful. The alternative is counter-productive. Penalising those in need of help forces them to have to make themselves appear less able, causes them to be reticent about coming off benefits for fear of never getting them back and is extremely detrimental to their long-term well-being.

6. Research and improvement

Shine a light on why so little is spent on mental health research, given the financial and life chance costs of mental illness. Do something serious and long lasting to reverse this. And then measure the impact longitudinally. No-one says we're spending too much on cancer research, do they? Use that as our benchmark.AND listen to the eminent Professor Don Berwick, who makes the point that inspection never improved any health system. We need to invest in improvement science, architecture and skills for the whole NHS, of which mental health is an intrinsic, integrated part. Calling something NHS Improvement doesn't necessarily make it an improvement body, by the way. But it is a good start.

I've shared these thoughts with the fabulous Paul Farmer, CE of Mind, who is leading one of three national task forces set up to help deliver the NHS England Five Year Forward View. The other two are on cancer and maternity care. I know he wants to do the best he can. But he needs your help.

If you are part of the mental health family, and I would argue that every human being should be, please join in. Let's increase

If I ruled the world....(cont.)

our ambition for those of us who experience mental illness, and focus hard on a small number of important things that will actually change lives. And then let's concentrate and not squabble amongst ourselves as we set about achieving them.

That's how winning teams win, against all the odds.

To update on that blog, the Mental Health Taskforce report, *The Five-Year Forward View for Mental Health* came out four months later than anticipated, in February 2016. It laid bare the shocking state of NHS mental health services, the disparity in what was available, the beds crisis in adult and children's mental health services, the long waits for therapy in many areas, the absence of any consistently organised response for people in a mental health crisis, and the unavailability of care for women with postnatal mental illness in many parts of the country.

The NHS England response seemed impressive. A large sum of money was reported to have been allocated. Or at least, a sum was named. But then it started to be widely disputed whether this was actually new money at all. And in May 2016, the excellent NHS Providers (previously known as the Foundation Trust Network) published a detailed report showing just how little of the new money promised to mental health services had been allocated. In fact, many trusts were being asked to make even greater savings and to disband essential services in the overall drive for efficiency, in most cases at levels greater than the savings meted out to other parts of the NHS. This demonstrated that the unfair discrimination towards mental health services was even more stark than people had realised.

All this continues to be possible because there are no national targets or standard reporting. And because no-one really cares enough.

I want to make it clear that I don't blame mental health commissioners nearly as much as it might appear. They are unfairly discriminated against too. Their allocations are rarely an annual proportion of the total commissioning budget. I know for a fact that they tend to get given what they got last year, minus a bit. They are harangued about making savings based on spurious notions of modernisation. And they are usually not nearly senior enough to be invited to the board table to argue the case for increased or even static investment to support positive service change and development.

I end this chapter with a version of something I wrote to launch the Time to Change project I chaired looking at stigma within mental health services. We reported in July 2016.[9]

No Them or Us. Just We

Some people call antidepressants 'happy pills'. I'm not keen on this description. In my experience, they slice the top and bottom from my emotional range and I feel neither happy nor sad.

Instead, they bring a calm which is welcome but can leave me feeling blunted, even flat. I know others describe similar effects.

Antidepressants helped me go back to work very quickly after my breakdown in November 2013. Skilled care from my psychiatrist and GP, timely psychological therapy and the kindness of colleagues helped even more. Plus an over-developed work ethic. For those lucky enough to have decent

---

[9] www.time-to-change.org.uk/about-us/about-our-campaign/professionals

No Them or Us. Just We (Cont.)

jobs, going back to work and feeling useful can play a big part in our recovery.

I mention this because I want you to understand my state of mind on 24th February 2014, six weeks after I went back to my job at the time, running a mental health trust. Going back to work was probably the hardest thing I have ever done; I have tried to explain why elsewhere in this book.

Anyway, on this particular day, I attended a round-table event arranged by Time To Change. Had I not been on my medication, I might have felt the need to challenge what we were being told. Or wept. Because I and the other NHS leaders present heard stuff at that meeting that we desperately wanted not to be true, and yet deep down we knew it to be so. It was like learning about institutional racism. Only this time, it was institutional stigma and discrimination from the services we were responsible for towards people who use our services.

We heard that, despite the measurable shifts in attitude of the general public, highlighted in July that year by Time to Change and again showing small but significant improvement, attitudes within the NHS have not shifted. In some cases, they have got worse. And the places where they appear most entrenched, as reported by those who know – patients - are within mental health services. This rang horribly true.

From this meeting was born a desire among a number of us to do something to change the situation. Five months later, at my retirement party, I listed some of the things I planned to do with my new found free time. One of them was to offer my services to Time to Change to help tackle this intrinsic issue within *mental health services. And although I planned to earn a modest living writing, speaking and coaching others, I wanted to do this work as a volunteer. I felt I had something to pay back.*

It has taken time to set up the project. But now it is well underway. Time to Change is working with two mental health trusts, 2Gether and Northumberland, Tyne and Wear. Like me, they are volunteers. The trusts were selected by us because they could demonstrate their readiness at the most senior level to address stigma within their own services with integrity, hard work and, most importantly for me, compassion.

On the working group, which I chair, we have reps from the two trusts, four experts by experience, our full-time project manager, senior colleagues from Rethink and Mind who together are responsible for running Time to Change, plus from time to time two people from a social research company who are carrying out work on attitude measurement.

You can read more about the purpose and details of the project on the Time to Change website www.time-to-change.org.uk.

Stigmatisation of those who need mental health support is alive and kicking within the NHS. It manifests itself with lack of empathy towards those who self-harm or are otherwise in crisis, as described in the CQC report into crisis care published in 2015; low expectations from clinicians about future prospects for people who experience serious mental illness; lack of investment in research into new treatments; marginalisation of mental health in the way the NHS is planned and organised; and unfair treatment of mental health services by local and national commissioners in their expectations and funding decisions.

No Them or Us. Just We (Cont.)

But I have high hopes. There is an absolute acceptance among those involved in our project that things need to change. Instead of simply asking people who work in mental health to be more compassionate, the change needs to start at the most senior level. We have sign-up for this work from the very top of NHS England, Mind, Rethink, Time to Change and at the trusts. And we agree that for staff to work respectfully with patients and treat them with optimism, expertise and compassion, they need to experience the same from their colleagues, including their most senior leaders, their commissioners and their regulators.

A long time ago I was told by a nurse that I was a waste of space and that looking after me after I had hurt myself took him away from patients who were truly deserving of his care. At the time, I absolutely believed him. It took me many years to unlearn what he said. And it nearly broke my heart to hear, at that meeting back in February 2014, that such attitudes are still relatively commonplace today.

The difference now is that we are talking about them. Acknowledging a problem is the first and most important step towards solving it.

Chapter 7

When things go wrong. And when leaders get judged

Introduction: decisions

Some people make decisions quickly. And some of us take longer. How you make decisions is not a measure of intellectual ability, but rather of personality type and preference. However, some people erroneously think that being quick witted is the equivalent of intelligence.

I am usually in the latter category: I need longer to decide about things, particularly if they are important. As a chief executive I have on occasions been forced to make my decisions too quickly. And in doing so, I have not always been confident about or even totally agreed with the decisions I reached. I mention decisions because it took a long time to make up my mind about how to tackle the subject matter of this chapter, which is about when things go wrong.

A book that helped me understand what was happening to me and many others within the NHS system that we had collectively created is *Intelligent Kindness* by John Ballatt and Penelope Campling [10]. I cannot commend their work more highly. The authors write with great wisdom and kindness about the current dilemmas that beset us over what to do when things go wrong. They say: *'The process of creating a culture that will nourish compassionate healthcare begins with daring to turn the focus from chasing poor practice and controlling people to supporting and enabling staff to do what they would in most cases want to do well…. A*

---

[10]www.rcpsych.ac.uk/usefulresources/publications/books/rcpp/9781908020048.aspx

compassionate healthcare culture depends on having the courage to trust the goodwill and skills of the majority, and the imagination to understand what they need to help them do their jobs well. Imagination is also required to understand the likely effects on staff and patients of any way of regulating and managing'. P 179

Special measures

As I started writing this chapter, the news emerged of two more hospital trusts and the first ambulance trust being placed in Special Measures. There were at that time around 30 such organisations. The idea behind these measures, created in 2013, is supposedly that the trusts concerned will get expert help and influence in order to bring about rapid but at the same time sustainable improvements.

In the case of one of those announced in 2015, East Sussex Healthcare, just along the coast from where I live, I think in all honesty they probably needed it. The staff there have struggled over money, workload and patient safety across two sites 20 miles apart for a number of years. There have been numerous unpopular plans to reorganise, which have been variously opposed by local politicians, patients and senior clinical staff. There had also been a rapid turnover of chief executives and by 2015 the latest iteration of the trust board appeared to have become beleaguered within their local system. The lack of connection, even antipathy, between the board at the trust and those who should be working in partnership with them in the CCGs and the local authorities was palpable within the local media. Their CQC inspections repeatedly produced an overall score of Inadequate, with return visits to check on progress apparently finding that the trust had not made significant improvements.

A change of leadership, while sad for those involved, was probably necessary; senior people in such very tough jobs get very tired. The constant demands can make them become defensive and unable to see the wood for the trees. And even if they manage to retain the necessary clarity of vision, how they are viewed by others casts a cloud over everything they do. It felt to me that they had earned a rest. Whether it all needed to be so bloody is quite another matter. The report looked at the trust in isolation, when it is very significantly reliant on the support of others to succeed. Whether this is fair or helpful is a subject that I will return to later.

Another trust that was put into Special Measures at the same time was Cambridge University Hospitals NHS Foundation Trust. This had many of us reeling. The board weren't given the benefit of a return CQC inspection; the initial report simply stated that they were Inadequate, and they were placed straight into Special Measures. And yet they apparently had world class outcomes for their specialist services, were reported to have an excellent safety record across most care groups, and staff were judged by the CQC themselves to give outstanding care in most areas.

The problems the trust faced included a large recurrent deficit, rising demand in numbers, complexity and acuity of patients needing emergency admission, and recruitment problems, particularly in nursing posts. But they were merely a forerunner; by 2018, these problems are shared by the majority of acute trusts across the country.

The most damning criticism that the CQC spokesperson seemed to be able to offer in a BBC Radio 4 *Today* programme interview on the day of the announcement was that the CEO Dr Keith McNeil, who had taken the honourable route and resigned the previous week, had a different vision for the organisation than some staff, in that he saw the trust's future as a specialist centre which also ran some local NHS services. Staff interviewed by the CQC thought of it as a district general hospital that also happened to run some specialist services.

In fact, it is both, and this may be the nub of the problem. Dr McNeil's very thoughtful interview with the local BBC after resigning was, in my view, an object lesson in self-awareness, humility and dignity. He said he had come to accept that he wasn't the person to tackle the issues faced by the trust, and that the new leader needed to have a more granular handle on the day-to-day operations than he had been able to achieve. That sounds more like the role of a chief operating officer than a chief executive, who is meant to develop the overall strategic direction and hold others to account for delivery. But it is what the CQC appeared to be asking for, and the board had apparently agreed. I imagine that, had they not, they would have found themselves going the same way as Dr McNeil.

A renowned heart surgeon such as Dr McNeil understands better than most the relationship between safety and being open about admitting mistakes. He had been one of the most measured and articulate of NHS chief executives, well-regarded by managers and clinicians, who appeared unafraid to say that what was being asked of acute trusts had become impossible, or close to impossible, unless the whole system is re-engineered and we reset our expectations.

Re-engineering the whole system is in effect what is being trialled via the vanguard sites that are being sponsored at the time of writing by NHS England. The fact that a world class heart surgeon turned chief executive could be unseated in the way Dr McNicholl was, only half way through a five year plan to turn an organisation round and before any attempts at a system reset had even been attempted, should fill us all with grave concern. Because, as the brilliant Professor Rosebeth Moss Kanter of Harvard Business School wrote in 2009:

'Welcome to the miserable middles of change. This is the time when Kanter's Law kicks in. Everything looks like a failure in the middle. Everyone loves inspiring beginnings and happy endings; it is just the middles that involve hard work.'[11]

---

[11] https://hbr.org/2009/08/change-is-hardest-in-the-middl

It seems to me, and I say this having spent many years puzzling over this conundrum, that we are going to have to talk much more openly with the public about what success and failure means within public services. Change will not be linear, nor will it appear to deliver success from Implementation Day One. With the growing demands of an ageing and thus more complex population, we have to decide what it is we all want from the healthcare system. There are almost infinite opportunities to intervene, which could make things better for the individual patient but, equally, could make them much worse. And each of these investigations and interventions uses more resources than doing nothing. Without this open discussion, the healthcare system will go on doing what it currently does, and we will have an increasing number of apparent failures.

We cannot rely on politicians to lead this discussion because too often they will stake their careers in defending the local status quo, and will never be able to imagine a horizon that is further away than the date of the next general election. Our political system as currently arranged is essentially about winning and losing. This gets played out in local as well as national politics. The NHS is much too important to be played around with like a political football. Yet that is what it has become.Nor, it seems to me, can we rely on regulators because they are capable of coming up with decisions such as the one made in Cambridge. I was among the group of NHS leaders who really wanted regulation to be different under the new CQC regime. And I still believe that it can be. And yet I watched the debate between people, including many much wiser than me, who have questioned the decision on Cambridge, and I've seen the CQC response, which seems to be that you just have to trust us, because we know we are right.

In the final chapter of *Intelligent Kindness*, Ballatt and Campling explain with precision and evidence why our current approach to regulation is not going to achieve the improvements envisaged. Indeed it will, in all probability, drive compassionate, high quality care backwards because the focus is on measuring compliance and uniformity rather than encouraging compassion, creativity and voluntary effort.

They wrote this in 2011. In 2018, it seems even more relevant.

How can we make things better?

Until the Putting People First conference held in Leeds in June 2015, I had only known John Walsh through social media. But I cannot thank him enough for inviting me to that conference. I met folk from the local NHS, voluntary sector and local authorities who shared an interest in helping vulnerable people.

I observed a groundswell of support for a very different way of being at work, where people bring their whole and unique selves to bear on issues that matter, where failure is seen as an opportunity for learning rather than a weakness to be vilified, and where treating patients/clients/service users with deep and real compassion is underpinned by working with love and compassion towards one another. Thanks also to all the organisers and speakers and to everyone else who was there. They were honest and kind, including when they challenged one another.

There is a large body of evidence that all staff, from cleaners to chief executives, provide better, safer, kinder care if they are encouraged to operate with integrity and openness. This stuff isn't new. Avedis Donabedian, who was born in Beirut in 1919 and died in Michegan in 2000, wrote wisely about improving the quality of healthcare before anyone else had thought of it, and published his world-famous framework in 1966. As well as being the father of improving quality in healthcare, he was also a poet. And he said this:

'Systems awareness and systems design are important for health professionals, but they are not enough. They are enabling mechanisms only. It is the ethical dimensions of individuals that are essential to a system's success. Ultimately, the secret of quality is love. You have to love your patient, you have to love your

profession, you have to love your God. If you have love, you can then work forward to monitor and improve the system.'[12]

Here's a precis of what I said at the conference about authentic leadership, building on what I had heard, and which seemed to go down quite well with a wise and thoughtful audience.

Bad things happen. Good leaders look after their people at such times. We live in a blame culture so this is very, very hard.

The more rules and procedures you impose, the less creative and compassionate your people will become. But resisting external demands to introduce even more can also be very hard.

We performance manage and inspect individual organisations at the expense of the collective system, and the patients who struggle across the myriad bits of the system. Moving to a more collective approach is a goal we could all agree on. But what about accountability, comes the cry. Or, who would we blame when things go wrong?

There is a leader in all of us, whether we are a patient or family member, work on reception or sit at the board room table. Work hard, if needs be against the grain, to be defined by what you do best, not by what scares you most.

Bring all of you to what you do. It took me far too long to learn that being all of me, including the bits I was less proud of, even ashamed of, made me a more authentic leader. Don't try to hide your imperfections like I did. It is an added burden. And things are hard enough already.

Many people are privately saying that everything now isn't right, and some measures intended to improve care are actually conspiring to make it less compassionate and safe.

---

[12] *http://qualitysafety.bmj.com/content/13/6/472*

If you agree with this, please find the courage to speak truth to power. This is what I am trying to do these days, via this book and in other ways. The more of us who do it, the harder it will be to either pick us off or ignore us.

My final thought is this. If you are in a leadership role and you see a colleague who is having a tough time, please don't metaphorically cross to the other side of the road as if they had contracted some toxic disease you are afraid you might catch. And please don't believe the awful things you read online, or even join in the anonymous bear-baiting that passes for acceptable online comment these days.

Instead, get in touch. Ask them how they are doing. Listen to them really carefully, without interrupting. And offer them your genuine support. Because you never know. One day, it could be you.

Chapter 8

It's got to be perfect: or has it? Making mistakes and learning from them

A few words of introduction

When I started writing this book, I knew there would be some parts of my story that I would shy away from. The ones about stuff that went wrong and in particular, instances that most sharply highlight my own failings and flaws. I knew I'd have to get there at some point. Memoirs that avoid such things are dishonest and, let's be frank, pretty boring.

As it turns out, I seem to have shared my mistakes pretty evenly throughout the book. This section is therefore a precis of the events that needed more space, or didn't quite fit anywhere else.

I get the impression from reviews – I haven't read all of their books, by the way - that leaders such as Sir Stuart Rose, Lord Sebastian Coe and Sir Alex Ferguson don't experience the misgivings or sleepless nights that I had. Sheryl Sandberg apparently does, but having admitted to getting things wrong, in her book *Lean In* she usually seems to find solutions that turn a disaster into a triumph. I like that she has now written about the mistakes she made in her first book *Lean In*, from her new perspective as a widow and single parent in her next book *Option B*.

Leaders who can admit their mistakes and grow from them, in the glare of publicity, are the ones who should succeed in our new, more open but ever more challenging world. I say should. But it doesn't yet feel that way.

In this chapter, I'm going to share some of my worst mistakes and try to be as truthful as I can about the lessons that, with hindsight, I have drawn from them. However, it isn't a misery memoir. There is always something to take away from grim experiences, if one can allow oneself the benefit of kindness and a bit of perspective. I'm working hard on both.

This is perhaps the part of the book that some of you will have jumped to. I will try not to disappoint. The list could of course be almost endless, because there is nothing I was involved with over those 13 years, or indeed the ones that preceded them that, on reflection, I couldn't have improved on. What I've tried to include here is a list of the occasions when, with the wonderful benefit of that seldom seen but invaluable instrument, the retrospectoscope, I have learned the most.

Invariably they also involved some pain along the way, and by no means all of it felt by me.

My first homicide enquiry publication

Setting aside balloons (see Chapter 2) my first big mistake coincided with the publication of a long-awaited homicide enquiry in early 2003. The tragic death of a young patient, in extremely unusual circumstances, had occurred in the late 1990s. Because of the nature of the case, it had received national media coverage, including sensationalist headlines and double-page spreads in various tabloid newspapers.

This had happened some years before I became the accountable officer, and so publication of the investigation report should have been relatively straightforward for me. All I had to do was show our truthful, heartfelt concern for the family, demonstrate that we had learned lessons from the findings in the report, and at the same time be clear that many things had changed since the time of the incident. It should also have been relatively low key.

However, I found myself allowing my relative inexperience and the heightened anxiety of others within and beyond the trust to make me stray from this path. There was an initial plan simply to publish the report on the SHA website. We moved from this to planning a high-profile press conference and hiring expensive media advisors without me really registering at the time how this had happened. This approach ramped up the anxiety levels of all concerned, and ensured that the publication got national attention. After all, the media advisers had to earn their not-insubstantial fee.

Despite not having commissioned the report, and struggling to understand fully its relevance and purpose, I then allowed myself to be pushed forward as the media spokesperson on behalf of all the relevant agencies. I don't regret the experience this brought. But I do wish I had felt more in control of the decisions taken at the time, and allowed myself pause for breath afterwards.

The night before publication of a high-profile enquiry such as this is invariably sleepless, which adds unhelpfully to the drama. On publication day itself, a time for sombre suits and faces, there were a few near-hysterical moments. One of the media advisors was themselves being pursued by a tabloid journalist because of a recent indiscretion with a high-profile TV personality; we had to provide them with a secret exit to avoid their own paparazzi. An uninvited, also high-profile spokesperson who was antagonistic towards us, arrived accompanied by a frail relative. This relative was left unattended in our reception area while filming with various national TV crews was underway. They became distressed and had to be comforted by the same staff who were at that moment being criticised on national television by the person who seemed to have abandoned them.

My own TV appearances seemed to go OK, and I was particularly pleased to be filmed live* by ITV inside one of our hospitals, a new one that had replaced the hospital that had come in for so much criticism in the report. A number of staff who had cared for the deceased patient were present. They had been traumatised by the extended enquiry process, and incensed that their efforts to keep the person safe over many years were not recognised by the report's authors. They watched as I fully accepted the criticisms in the report but also went out of my way to commend the compassion and endeavours of the staff.

My mistake was in allowing publication of the report to become all-consuming which undoubtedly distracted us from what the findings really meant AND from the day-to-day business of running the trust. And in particular, I failed to capitalise on that moment. It is all too easy after an exhausting media circus to breathe a sigh of relief and then return quickly back to 'normal'.

In fact, such events provide an opportunity to set a new normal. I should have ensured that we embarked on further work with the affected staff immediately after publication. That might have helped them, me and my senior team, to recognise that we had much more to learn from the report findings than were apparent on first reading it.

Compassion fatigue can occur even in the best services, especially with complex cases such as this one which can challenge and split teams. The care given, while full of effort from all involved, had not been fit for purpose. We needed a total redesign of the care pathway for people with Borderline Personality Disorder, which was achieved eventually but not until a number of years later.

And finally, everyone concerned was traumatised, and I know I failed to recognise that. And I include myself in that list.

---

*Why to opt for a live TV or radio interview whenever possible

As my broadcast experience increased, I grew to prefer live broadcasts to recorded pieces. In a recorded item, whatever question you are asked, you must learn to keep repeating yourself so that they can't cut your output and somehow contrive to make you look uncaring or complacent. I've had the experience where the one and only thing I wished I hadn't said was used in a broadcast, and it is pretty humiliating, especially

---

> *when your friends and colleagues contact you afterwards to ask*
> *why you said this but didn't say that.*
> *Although it may feel like peering down the barrel of a gun to do*
> *a live interview, you are free to say what you want on TV or*
> *radio and know that you are getting your most important points*
> *across.*
> *And finally, live interviews give you a massive shot of adrenalin*
> *which, if you manage to control it, makes the experience feel*
> *less like being ritually tortured and provides a much better*
> *opportunity to be yourself and avoid sounding like an uncaring*
> *management-speak clone.*

How not to build a new mental hospital

In the summer of 2001, I asked to be shown round the services that were coming together to form the new West Sussex mental health trust the following year. As the project director, I said I wanted to meet staff and patients and see the facilities so that I could do a good job.

But as I've said in Chapter 1, I had an ulterior motive. I wanted to see what things were really like because I was going through my internal decision-making process about whether to apply for the chief executive job myself. And I wanted to be sure I knew what I was letting myself in for.

I was aware that the services the new trust would inherit from the north of the county were in poorer shape than those along the South Coast, due to historical funding differences. Those long-ago discriminatory investment decisions had a profoundly negative impact on people who needed help from mental health services. For example, one of the three large Victorian mental hospitals that served Sussex[13], St Francis in Haywards Heath, was closed in the early 1990s. The imposing main hospital building plus all the land and other buildings suitable for development were sold, and the NHS netted some significant capital receipts.

But instead of this money being spent to improve mental health care, it was used to build the Princess Royal Hospital in Haywards Heath[14].

At the time, it seemed that few had noticed the losses from mental health. The rump of services that remained after St Francis closed were allocated to an ugly little block at Horsham Hospital called, ironically, Rose Ward, and a notoriously awful 1960s eyesore of a building at the back of the Princess Royal called, even more ironically, The Villa.

Crawley, a new town in the North of West Sussex with the highest ethnicity and morbidity, had no mental health beds at all. It did have a day hospital, a very good service provided from the dampest and most dilapidated portacabin I have ever visited.

I remember my first visit to Rose Ward. You could feel the menacing atmosphere as soon as you entered. The design was all wrong. It

---

[13] You can read about all three Sussex Victorian asylums, plus the other smaller learning disability hospitals, in a lovely little book written by Adam Trimingham called *Out of the Shadows*, published in 2006 by Pomegranate Press.

[14] Many believed when it was built that The Princess Royal Hospital was a white elephant acute hospital in the wrong place, with the location chosen for personal and political reasons rather than public benefit. But having had my gall bladder removed there with great skill and wonderful care from all concerned in 2011, had I ever thought that to be so, I no longer agree. It is an excellent hospital, part of the wonderful, often unfairly criticised Brighton and Sussex University Hospitals NHS Trust.

was gloomy and cramped, with low ceilings. There were four crowded sleeping bays, each for six people, and not enough bathrooms, circulation or day space for there to be any possibility of separating patients according to gender or need. The so-called relaxation room was thick with smoke and populated by people who seemed to have nothing to do with the hospital, children in buggies and several large dogs. The staff were too frightened to ask these visitors to leave, and the ward sister was at her wit's end to stop the drug dealing that was openly occurring on the ward. She had tried to institute a locked door policy, but come up against severe criticism from the Mental Health Act Commission because most of the patients at that time were not detained and therefore it was believed detrimental to their rights and wellbeing to lock them in. This meant that the drug dealers could also not be locked out.

Rose Ward was bad enough. But it was my visit to The Villa that had me sitting in my car afterwards with my head in my hands. There were just two sleeping areas, one for 15 women and one for 15 men, plus a couple of tiny side rooms. The beds were so close together that there was only just enough space for a locker between them. We entered the women's end and I noticed a lady rocking on her bed, keening in despair. As a visitor I should not have been able to see this. But the flimsy bed curtains were too short and gave no privacy. It was hot and stuffy, not helped by the windows having been screwed shut 'for safety reasons'. A local builder had gone out of business while fixing some broken toilets; they were now taped off with hazard warnings, leaving only two that still worked, to be shared by 32 male and female patients, located in the only two bathrooms. The day room was bleak and dank, and the staffing levels inadequate, further depleted by one member of staff who was required to sit on sentry duty by the main door at the top of the stairs with a list to sign people in and out, apparently because the lock was defective and there was no reception to oversee the entrance. The staff had a list of complaints for me but these were all about their own conditions rather than those experienced by the patients.

So what to do? I found myself vowing inwardly that I would get that chief executive job, and shut those two terrible places as soon as I possibly could. If I could not bear the thought of being cared for there myself or for a member of my family to be looked after there, how could it possibly be OK for anyone else?

Roll forward to October 2002 and The Hawth Theatre, Crawley. We held an *Any Questions*-style public event attended by 350 people. In response to a question about Rose Ward and why there were no impatient facilities in Crawley, I found myself promising that we would close it, and The Villa, and build a brand-new hospital in Crawley instead. Had I said the same thing in Haywards Heath or Horsham, I doubt I would have got the standing ovation I received for my answer. But I knew my audience. My chair, Glynn Jones, whispered 'Now you've done it' and I realised I had been rash. But with Simon Robbins, chief executive of Surrey and Sussex SHA also on the panel applauding as loudly as everyone else, I knew I had an ally.

Getting that hospital built took considerable work. I still don't know where I found the belief that we would do it, given the state of the finances we had inherited (more on this in the next section). Sometimes it is better not to know what lies ahead, or leaders would never dream of doing anything difficult at all.

Once I had managed to extricate us from the possibility of taking over a wing of the 1970s built Crawley Hospital, which would have been even worse than Rose Ward, we had to find a large enough building plot where we stood a chance of getting planning permission to build a state of the art mental hospital. This is not the kind of development most people welcome at the bottom of their gardens.

Not to mention £16 million to actually build the thing.

Some 'thank you's'

I need to thank quite a few people for helping us make that hospital a reality. There was Spencer Prosser, our Director of Finance who combined a laconic sense of humour with being a genius at writing and presenting business cases, with a secret passion for helping vulnerable people. And Mark Heathcote, Director of Estates, who saw the delivery of this building as the culmination of his career and turned a hospital that could have been just OK into a thing of beauty. Sue Morris, Locality Director for West Sussex, was a very charming terrier for ensuring we met the needs and aspirations of patients, staff and visitors. Ralph Hayward was the best mental health commissioner I have ever worked with, and he knew that we needed to balance the right number of beds with an expansion of community services. He was no pushover, but a wonderful ally. John Dixon, Director of Social Services, a dear friend to the trust, made it possible for us to buy the land from West Sussex County Council, and Ann Beales of the CAPITAL project, representing people who used our service, argued the case for turning a school site into a mental hospital so eloquently that the sale went through without a hitch. Michael Coughlin, chief executive of Crawley Borough Council, taught me that working with elected members was so much better than inadvertently annoying them. And the three ward councillors, David Shrieves, Brenda Smith and Jim Smith plus the local MP Laura Moffatt listened carefully to us and set politics aside for the greater good of the wider community. There are so many more people who were part of the project, but the final person I will mention is Natalie Cadman, our project officer and until recently, Matron at the hospital. Natalie shared my vision that mental hospitals are not places where most of us ever need to go, but for those who do, they should be sanctuaries of safety, calm and healing. And as I hope this chapter demonstrates, achieving this has by no means been easy

There were many objections to overcome before we eventually acquired a site previously occupied by an old school in Langley Green, Crawley early in 2005, and started planning in earnest.

Nonetheless, Langley Green Hospital, one of six acute mental hospitals serving a population of 1.6 million across West Sussex, Brighton and Hove, and East Sussex, was officially opened by Professor Louis Appleby CBE, National Clinical Director for Mental Health, on 16th September 2008. Louis joked that he had flown from Manchester to Gatwick, and at the airport had seen Robinho, a footballer who had just been transferred from Real Madrid to Manchester City for £32.5 million. For that money, he said, you can either buy one footballer or build two mental hospitals. Louis also kindly said it was the most beautiful hospital he had ever seen, and held to that view over a number of years.

But after we had opened, there was something not quite right. None of us could quite put our finger on it, but the atmosphere was not as positive as we had hoped. Despite my personal efforts and those of members of my team to help local clinicians and managers to capitalise on the engagement work we had started while building the hospital, there was a sense of us and them between the hospital and the local community. There were excellent meeting spaces upstairs which could be used to host events to help put the hospital on the map. And yet senior staff at the hospital seemed hostile towards these efforts. We had some worrying complaints about staff attitudes which proved difficult to address, and recruitment to clinical positions was problematic, despite the proximity to public transport, free parking and the superb facilities.

Perhaps the most tangible sign that all was not right was the café, designed so carefully to be right at the front of the hospital so that it could be used by members of the local community as well as visitors to the hospital, as well as patients and staff. But it always seemed to be shut. Various attempts with directly employed staff, volunteers and via a third sector partner were to no avail. There was a parade of local shops around the corner, and patients would go there instead for a coffee or to buy takeaways.

In his first novel *The Rachel Papers*, Martin Amis introduces the notion of a rotating worry-list. In short, unless you never suffer from anxiety, you will always be worrying about something. When something bad happens, whatever that is will push your previous top worry further down the list and thus it will receive less of your attention.

In the four years after it opened, Langley Green Hospital occasionally reached the top of my worry list, but more often than not, a serious incident elsewhere, the potential loss of a contract via yet another tendering exercise, or a worrying complaint would get higher listing.

And so it took a truly terrible incident in August 2012 with a sickening twist in the tail to make me and my team realise that things at Langley Green needed to change. This incident has received much public attention, so I can report it here. In summary, two patients left one of the wards at the hospital, met a third at the local shops, agreed to buy some illegal drugs, the first two then travelled by public transport to a flat belonging to one of them to use the drugs, whereupon a fight ensued and one stabbed the other to death.

This was a tragedy for all concerned; they were in our care; a life was tragically lost and another life ruined. We set about reviewing the case, cooperating fully with the police and the coroner. But there was worse to come. Having reported the incident to the police, ten days later it emerged that the most senior doctor and the four most senior nurses at the hospital, on hearing about the incident, had not reported it immediately. Instead, they met in secret, looked through the notes of both patients and decided, in the light of the incident, to collude together to alter the records in order to make the care of both patients seem more optimal than it had been. And where they changed the records, they forged the signatures of more junior staff, thereby implicating those staff also. They did this knowing that the records would shortly be sequestered by the police and would be used in court by the coroner and in any criminal proceedings. They were therefore prepared to perjure themselves in order to cover up any perceived failings.

Eventually, one of the nurses confessed; she said she could not live with her conscience, although given they had made a mistake and signed one of the records in the name of someone who hadn't in fact been on duty that day, it was perhaps the fear of discovery that led to the confession. The others maintained that they believed that they had to do it or they would have been in deep trouble. Eventually some were dismissed and some resigned. They were either removed from their professional registers or voluntarily removed themselves.

Only one appealed against dismissal; the mitigation they gave for doing what they did was that the trust would have sanctioned them had the paucity of care been known. This person, a nurse with over 20 years experience, could give no examples of others who had got into such trouble. But it was clearly what they believed. They said they had no choice but to falsify the records. And they also showed the opposite of compassion for the patients, whose drug-taking they blamed for the awful events that occurred. I had one of my sleepless nights after hearing this appeal.

This is a shocking story. But my point in telling it is not to shock you about the events per se. All five of these staff had worked for us for many years. The majority had worked at the hospitals that preceded Langley Green. When a patient was admitted or a visitor arrived, they didn't meet me or one of my executive team. They met staff on the wards, who were led by these five people. They set the tone and the culture at that hospital. And despite all the things that we said to our senior staff and directly to frontline staff about anyone being able to make a mistake and the most important thing is always to tell the truth, they somehow believed that covering their own backs mattered more than anything else, that 'the trust' was punitive and that it was them against us.

Had I been a better leader, I believe I could and should have read the warning signs and somehow uncovered the problems at this hospital before something so shocking as altering records after an incident took place. Had I listened more carefully, I feel I should somehow have been able to find out that group-think had developed among this senior team which saw some patients as more deserving than others, and 'the trust' as an unhelpful bogeyman to pit your wits against and keep at a distance, rather than a supportive employer who wanted every member of staff to do their best, and a caring provider whose primary purpose was to help patients lead the fullest possible lives.

I could go on. This has been extremely hard to write. I will forever be deeply sorry that so many patients and staff were affected. And I wish everyone who works at Langley Green Hospital good luck in their ongoing efforts to create an open, compassionate and just culture, and offer them all my continued love and best wishes for the future.

Name badges

I am indebted to Dr Kate Granger whose *Hello, My Name Is...* campaign achieved what I failed to do despite 13 years of trying, which is to help NHS staff understand why wearing a name badge and introducing yourself to patients and colleagues matters so much.

At least, she has achieved it in some places, but by no means all. Kate had terminal cancer, yet still worked tirelessly with her husband Chris Pointon on the campaign as a volunteer. She did this on top of her day job as an NHS consultant until her cancer meant that she had, with great reluctance and sadness, to retire. She knew from her own ongoing experience as a patient that it is a continual struggle, and that people who say they are committed to *Hello, My Name Is...* one day can forget to use it the very next time they meet someone because they are stressed or feel too busy. For all those who have signed up to the campaign and say how much they love it, there are others who haven't even heard of it, or are like a small number of the people I used to lead, feel irritated or even insulted by something they see as trivial or obvious.

One doctor once said to me: 'The thing is Lisa, I don't work in Tesco and so I am not prepared to wear a plastic name badge.' This was more insulting to people who work in supermarkets than it was to me. But it is how a small proportion of NHS staff still feel.

Another clinician once emailed me after I had promoted the campaign in my weekly message and said this: 'I am insulted to think that you think that we don't introduce ourselves to our patients.'

I hadn't said that, of course, just suggested that teams might want to think about adopting the *Hello, My Name Is*….campaign. Because patients had told us time and again that they didn't know the name of the person treating them. Maybe if I had asked a clinician to lead it, it might have been more effective?

When chairing meetings, I like to go around the table and ask people to introduce themselves. Sometimes I also ask them to say something that relates to the subject matter of the meeting. It helps if everyone speaks at the outset, particularly for the shyer people who may never find their voice at all if they aren't encouraged to speak early on. Some people think this is a bit trite and respond when it is their turn with something like 'Oh, everyone knows me'.

But actually, this apparent self-effacement can be big-headed. It is also often wrong. It can be that there are people present who don't know them. And also, it is possible to forget people's names, especially in a stressful situation such as a meeting, let alone a hospital appointment. Being reminded gives people confidence.

It is even more important in mental health services. Imagine being a confused person who is having hallucinations or hearing voices, or whose memory and cognition is affected by dementia or another neurological condition. How unkind to expect people under such stress to be able to work out who is a patient and who is a member of staff, when everyone looks the same and no-one is wearing a uniform. Imagine being a desperately worried visitor, and wanting to know who to go to for help, but not being able to tell who the nurse in charge is, or to recognise a doctor you met once but only for a few minutes in circumstances where you had other more pressing things on your mind. Name badges and polite, regular introductions really do help.

I started talking about the importance of name badges back in January 2002, and banged on about them in my regular messages and at our monthly meetings with senior leaders until I retired in 2014. I had at least five myself, so that even if I had left one on a jacket I wasn't wearing that day or in another handbag, I could still be sure of wearing my name badge at work. For members of my team who lost them, I bought more. For teams I visited whose manager appeared not to have got the memo about everyone wearing a badge, I arranged for their badges to be ordered. And I collected name badge excuse stories.

Once I visited a ward where most of the staff were badgeless. My visit had been arranged for quite some time, and staff had made various efforts to placate me with home-made badges, including one nursing assistant who created hers from a clear plastic filing cabinet label attached to her bosom with Sellotape, a torn-off yellow post-it note and her name written in a pen that had apparently run out half way through and so was finished in pencil. If she hadn't asked me so seriously if I liked her badge, I would have thought it was a wind-up. When I spoke to the manager afterwards, he said they didn't have a budget for badges, and when I explained that they cost 70p each and anyway, it was a centralised budget, he admitted that he didn't know how to order them. Shortly afterwards, this ward was nominated in a beautiful citation by a patient for a regional award for compassion, which they won. There is no question that they were providing great care. But I still think they needed badges.

Another time, I met a team I am also not in any way criticising. They were clearly dedicated and hardworking. Their roles meant that they were unlikely to meet patients very often, if at all. Of the 20 members, only a handful had badges, and these were very old ones. The meeting was a celebration of something good that had recently happened, and so I waited until I saw their manager later to raise the matter of them not wearing badges. And the manager, who was a regular attender at our monthly briefings where badges had been discussed frequently, replied that these staff didn't need them, because they didn't meet patients or the public. And I said, but they meet staff and each other, and the manager very graciously accepted my point, and I am told immediately placed the order for badges.

I feel so sad that for all those preceding years, this team didn't think they were important enough to be entitled to have their own name badge.

My key learning points from this:

- Going on about something doesn't make it happen. It risks making it your issue rather than a collective one
- People who work in mental health are by nature non-conformers. Show them what they perceive to be a petty rule and they will find a way around it. They may also try to make you feel bad for insulting them by trying to implement it. And sometimes they will succeed
- Principles are great. But if you don't sort out the practicalities (like how to get the bloody badges) stuff won't happen
- You have to be even more explicit than you might think. For example, everyone needs a badge. That means everyone. There are no exceptions

- Maybe name badges, unless carefully introduced, can be seen as a barrier between staff and patients? Or they can be turned into one by people who are antagonistic about something deeper, but feel unable to express it?

Just as a follow-up to this and to link with the previous section on how not to build a hospital, another uphill struggle more successfully surmounted was getting staff name boards introduced onto every ward. In 2002, staff in some of the places we inherited when we set up the West Sussex trust were horrified at the thought of such a thing. They didn't want patients to know their surnames or even their job titles. Some went to the trouble of removing their photo and name from the early versions of these name boards, or even defacing them.

Now, staff name boards are seen as standard good practice in mental health care.

On the award-winning ward I mentioned earlier, I saw a beautifully executed staff board, with details about where each staff member had trained, their professional interests, some personal details and even in some cases photos of their pets. The patients clearly loved it, because it made the staff human and accessible and there was less of a sense of them and us.

Becoming a foundation trust

And so to a period in my career that had considerable ups and downs and from which I will draw a few lessons that I hope will be unexpected, even to those most closely involved.

First of all, the backstory. We launched West Sussex Health and Social Care NHS Trust in 2002 with those equine-unfriendly balloons mentioned in Chapter 3, and people were still saying how large and remote the trust was. But even as we did so, I was privately thinking that, if we were to achieve foundation trust status, still relatively new for mental health trusts at that stage, and develop specialties in which we could excel for our patients in service, teaching and research, we would need considerably more resources and a greater critical mass.

I recall sharing a gloomy moment in that first year with Spencer Prosser, my finance director, in the chilly little kitchen near my office. We perched together on the windowsill and faced our first Christmas with a dwindling supply of cash in the bank and the possibility of not being able to meet the January payroll. We both knew we had been sold a pup, in the sense that our income was less than our expenditure to the tune of circa 10 per cent. If we were to survive with our careers intact, we had to do something quickly.

And so we agreed that Spencer's job was to make a plea to Barry Elliott, the Director of Finance at Surrey and Sussex Strategic Health Authority, for several millions of bail-out money to buy us time to introduce some more permanent fixes. And mine was to make the case to Simon Robbins, chief executive of the SHA, that we knew what we were doing and had a more robust long-term strategic goal. Spencer devised a ten-point recovery plan, which we kept in a blue folder because blue was a positive colour. And I went to get advice from Duncan Selbie, who was then running another SHA in South East London, on what to do to persuade Simon. Duncan did me a little calculation to show that the NHS wasn't about to run out of cash, and that therefore I could push hard for the help we needed.

Armed with this calculation in the back of my notebook, the blue folder plus some vague thoughts of merger, I had a meeting with Simon. As usual, he wrote expansively all over his whiteboard, and the seeds of our plans to achieve teaching trust status and become Sussex Partnership were born.

It wasn't exactly Christmas Eve 2002 when the call came through from Barry, although in reminiscing, Spencer and I like to tell each other that it was. But it was the most welcome £3.5 million I have ever received, because it meant we could pay our staff, cover all our other costs and keep services safe while we sorted out the deficit properly and got ourselves onto an even footing.

I started discussing the reasons for the merger with my team and the board the following year, 2003. They thought it was exciting. And it became even more so as we began working with our partner trust in East Sussex early in 2004. A plan was developed with the SHA and our two boards that, because the other trust was by then without a chief executive, I should step in and run both trusts from January 2005 – April 2006, leading the merger at the same time.

That was probably the hardest working year of my life. I had two boards and two chairs who were about as different as two people could be, which would have been a useful plot device had I been writing this story as a novel. I suffered from what I used to pretend was a tug of love, but it was probably more about each wanting their fair dibs of chief executive time.

Actually, they got very good value because although my salary went up a bit, it wasn't even as much as my predecessor in East Sussex had earned. And I worked my socks off.

For those fifteen months, I led a larger than usual team, with some people working in West Sussex, some in East Sussex, and some being in a central core team with me. And I appointed a project director, Ann Merricks, the steadiest person I could possibly have chosen, who negotiated our way through the merger with wonderful tact and diplomacy.

The hardest part was persuading a third party, South Downs Health, over whom we had no authority, to release their mental health and related services to become part of the new trust. They did not agree, and I know there are people to this day who believe that I destroyed something wonderful for a personal vanity project.

They were wrong, and those services have fared better because of the merger than they might otherwise have done, although it has by no means always been plain sailing.

The chief executive post for the new trust did not have my name on it. I could have argued that I and others who were affected by the changes should get first crack at applying for the new posts. But in order to try to stop people saying that it was all about me and my West Sussex team taking over the world, I insisted that the job should be advertised nationally.

On the day of the interviews, I remember walking across one of our main sites to the interview room, feeling every eye upon me. It was one of the most exposing moments of my career. I got that job in January 2006, but it just felt like a relief and nowhere near as thrilling as the time I was a rank outsider and got appointed against the odds back in 2001.

The trouble with a hard 15 months like that is that there is no break before the next part starts. On Day 99 you are doing the old job. But Day 100 = Day 1 and you are immediately doing the new one.

The first thing we were asked to consider was our plan to achieve foundation trust status as well as deliver some massive savings to our commissioners, a time when they were ostensibly still meant to be investing in mental health services. And we were also building new hospitals, running services as well as trying to maintain contracts and win new ones.

Roll forwards to 7 July 2008, and our interview with the regulator Monitor, known as a board-to-board. This was the culmination of another 18 months of gruelling work, including a bruising practice board-to-board with the SHA when they told us we were in effect pretty useless and would never achieve FT status - or that was what I heard anyway. In addition, a five-year strategic plan had to be developed and tested to destruction with all sorts of ghastly downside scenarios and mitigated downside scenarios. We had visits from the SHA, management consultants appointed by the SHA, management consultants appointed by Monitor and management consultants appointed by us to help us prepare for all the other management consultants. In such circumstances, you begin to doubt whether you know your own name. And even if you know it, is it really your name and can you prove it please, with three sets of independently verified evidence. And a 20-point mitigation plan just in case.

I will always be grateful to Jenny Procter, a lovely manager working with Ann Merricks, who had again agreed to run the project. A week or so before we were due to go to Monitor, Jenny asked if she could have 15 minutes with me. I think I was showing the signs of fraying, as were others in my team. And she said something really kind: 'I probably shouldn't say this, but I'm going to say it anyway. You lot don't know just how good you are.'

Jenny's words really helped. The opening presentation I had been preparing for the Monitor session was dumped, and I produced something much more interesting and truthful about who we really were. I also ran it past all of our board members several times, and got them to critique the contents and how I planned to deliver it.

One of the more difficult parts of the preparation process was to recognise that Monitor were, rightly or otherwise, looking for business skills and experience among our non-executive directors that we simply didn't have. We had to part company with several very good people, which was painful, and our chair Pam Oates nobly stepped aside to become a non-executive director again, a role she performed with integrity and skill for several more years.

When our new chair John Bacon CB first met us, it was the end of March 2008 and we were deeply into the assessment with Monitor. John told us that these things were always challenging, and therefore it would be much better to do well and get through first time, because we might not get a second chance. Which was motivating in a kind of way.

What John didn't tell us was that he would invariably know and be respected by the majority of the Monitor panel members who would be assessing us. It helped but also added to the pressure to perform. On the day itself, we assembled far too early in a hotel near the Monitor offices. We had organised breakfast, but not many of us ate it.

To improve my mental attitude, I had decided to view my presentation as opening the batting for the team, rather than being the first one to ascend the steps of the gallows. This helped me stop thinking about myself, but it increased my feeling of responsibility.

To add further to the drama, the trust team we bumped into on their way out looked like they had just emerged from a street fight from which they had come off worst. Their session apparently hadn't gone well. The chief executive, who I knew, whispered to me a question that had apparently floored them, concerning something called head room. What the hell is head room, I hissed at Spencer. I don't know, he hissed back, surplus maybe? And in we went.

It wasn't an auspicious intro. But as I started a presentation that I had prepared so thoroughly that I could almost watch myself giving it, I noticed everyone relaxing. That advice from Ruth Carnall that I mentioned back in Chapter 2 about putting the panel at their ease seemed to be working. Everyone in our team seemed calm and well-informed. I can honestly say that the majority of us enjoyed our one and a half hours in there. I felt sorry when it was over, although I was more than relieved to be able to change out of my new very high heels and put on the back-up pair that one of the team had thoughtfully carried for me in her handbag.

And on 30 July 2008, right in the middle of our AGM, which was being broadcast across three sites to reduce the need for people to travel, I was called out to take a phone call from Stephen Hay at Monitor. We had passed and could call ourselves Sussex Partnership NHS Foundation Trust. And we had achieved a first, becoming a teaching trust at the same time.

But again, there was no gap.

All those management consultants and a bit of success can turn your head. We decided to stop meeting as a board in public every month, as our meetings with governors were in public and that felt sufficient public scrutiny now we were supposedly more independent. This seriously annoyed our commissioners, despite none of them ever actually attending our meetings. We instituted an internal business plan called *We Mean Business* to help us become more efficient. which grated with some of our clinicians. And we decided to get more aggressive with our commissioners who were asking for even more savings that we knew were unreasonable. But we couldn't defend our position effectively because we didn't trust them enough to share detailed activity information for fear they would simply ask for more savings.

During the subsequent year, we went on to have one or two worrying incidents plus conversations with people whose wisdom we valued and which brought me and the team back down to earth with a bump. We jettisoned the *We Mean Business* stuff because we realised it jarred with our culture.

Instead, we got to work on two parallel strategies that suited us much better which we called *Better by Design*, which was our strategic plan for services, and *Better by Experience*, about our culture and values. And we reinstituted meeting in public, despite the faff involved, because it clearly mattered to people, even to those who never turned up or even appeared to read our minutes.

The lessons I would take from reorganisation and becoming a foundation trust are these:

- You are better than you think when you are judging yourself harshly
- But probably not as good as you think are when you get too much up yourself. In other words, pride comes before a fall
- Do the right thing strategically. Just don't ever expect people to thank you for it

- After a big tournament, you need to rest your team, otherwise you won't succeed at the next one. You may even miss what you are actually meant to be there for in the first place, as I did for a few months back in 2008
- When you are giving a 45-minute potentially career-defining presentation, by all means dress the part, but wear comfortable shoes. My Monitor pair cost £199 and I wore them once. I sold them later on eBay for £95. You can do the cost-in-use calculation.

Chapter 9

Pride or prejudice?

Introduction

Pride is an interesting concept. For some it has negative connotations, with pride coming before a fall. Others use the word with great pride.

It is certainly true that some leaders can come over as rather boastful, crowing that 'I' did this or that, when clearly the efforts made were not theirs alone, or even theirs at all. And sometimes when the thing being boasted about is not even all that good anyway.

I don't want to risk appearing like that. But I also want to provide some balance in this book, and talk about the things that I did, always with others, for which I feel we have earned a collective right to feel pride. So here are a few examples, with lessons drawn on why these particular cases retain resonance for me now.

None of them were plain sailing. Each one had their 'difficult middles'[15]. But that's what makes them all the more worthy of celebration.

Equality, diversity and human rights

I've always been drawn to choose the less travelled path, and to support the underdog. It is in my nature. It led to me choosing to run a mental health trust, rather than the more obvious choices of acute or community services, given my most recent background prior to applying. I saw the job as being mainly about achieving equality for people who had for too long experienced stigma and

---

[15] See reference to Rosebeth Moss Kanter, in Chapter 7 of this book

unfair discrimination. It was my idea to commission the sign outside our headquarters early in my CE career that reads:

- **Positive about mental health.**
- **Fighting stigma**.

It underpinned our strategic and operational plans throughout my time in the job. I feel pleased, when I travel along the A27, to see that it is still there today.

However, what you say is all very well. What you do must be in synchrony.

In 2007, the Healthcare Commission, predecessor of the Care Quality Commission, contacted Sussex Partnership about a race equality review they planned to carry out into our systems and processes. I remember feeling quite offended by this. We had a diverse workforce, served some diverse communities and we really cared about race equality. Why did we need to be singled out for such a review?

We never learned whether we had been referred because someone somewhere had identified a problem, or whether we were seen to be doing things that might set a good example. Or if the selection was simply random.

Whichever it was, the findings were telling. We discovered that, while we had articulated good intentions at a senior level, these were not borne out through our policies and practices. We had some evidence to demonstrate that we took this aspect of equality seriously. But it was limited. And we didn't really know whether our black and minority ethnic patients or staff experienced stigma or discrimination in our services.

After licking my wounds and supporting others to do likewise, we decided to sort ourselves out. I agreed with the executive team that we needed to bring in race equality expertise, and we appointed an interim equalities manager who reported directly to me for three months. He worked with me and members of the executive team to start the legwork needed to put our aspirations about all aspects of equality, including race equality, into practice.

Our initial analysis made us realise that we had to invest further, in money but even more so in effort and attention. And this was how our small but highly effective Equality, Diversity and Human Rights Team came into being. I chaired the steering group, from its creation in 2007 until I retired in 2014, and we appointed an overall executive lead for equality, plus executive leads for each of the different equality strands. The work programme included revising the majority of our policies and procedures, embedding impact assessments into our change programme, making equality and human rights an essential part of our suite of training events, including for the executive team and the board, and introducing monitoring systems to find out what we needed to know about the people we served and our staff.

None of this happened overnight. And there were hiccups along the way, including times when senior colleagues questioned the need for quite so rigorous impact assessments, whether the resources being invested were giving us a real return on investment, and why the equalities team couldn't do all the work themselves but were instead intent on making equality part of everyone's business. And why I was personally so committed to this particular agenda. But we stuck with it, and managed to persuade others to stick with us as well.

In January 2012, we achieved an NHS first, achieving fourth place overall in the highly prestigious Stonewall Workplace Equalities Index. This was the first time an NHS organisation had made it into the top five places of the index, and meant that Sussex Partnership became the most highly recommended place to work in the NHS for Lesbian, Gay and Bisexual people. And although the index looks mainly at equality for this particular group, it measures systems and processes which apply to people from all groups who may experience stigma or discrimination from time to time.

The following year, 2013, we did even better – second place. Other NHS organisations did well too, including several for whom members of our equalities team had provided consultancy services. I have thanked many people for this work in the past. Here I will just mention Scott Durairaj, who led our small team and taught me that there can be no quality without equality. And Vincent Badu, our lead director, who was calm and resolute along a path that was not always smooth. Finally, Adam Churcher started out as the most junior member of the team and ended up leading it with expertise and good humour.

My favourite day came in 2013 when we held a celebratory event with our Black and Minority Ethnic Staff Network. As well as hearing from members of the network, and sharing delicious food prepared by staff with cultural links to the Indian Subcontinent, South Asia, Africa, the Caribbean and Eastern Europe, we welcomed a very special guest. The Reverend Mpho Tutu, daughter of Archbishop Desmond Tutu, addressed us and spent some very precious time talking in private with us. Together the Archbishop and Reverend Mpho run the international Tutu Foundation. They teach the principles of Ubuntu, used during the Peace and Reconciliation Commission in South Africa. Later that evening, some of our staff, including two of our directors who had completed mediation training at the Tutu Foundation, attended a meeting with Archbishop Tutu in London. I have never felt so proud or so humbled.

Archbishop Tutu and Reverend Mpho Tutu have written many books. The one I love, which Reverend Mpho signed for me, is *Made for Goodness*[16]. It says there is good in us all, whatever mistakes we have made or wrongs we have committed. It is full of hope and has helped me in the latter part of my career a great deal.

If I had my time again, I would definitely repeat the attention I gave to equality, diversity and human rights. It undoubtedly helped

---

[16] www.penguin.co.uk/books/1086561/made-for-goodness/

make our services better and provided a framework to challenge our own actions or inaction in relation to groups who experience disadvantage.

But I would add another aspect, were I doing the job today. We now have incontrovertible evidence that people who use mental health services experience stigma not only from members of the public, but also from staff who provide such services. This is manifest in downright cruelty in a small but unacceptable number of cases. But more frequently, in low expectations, lack of respect for the person's wishes, and a lack of hopefulness about future prospects.

As I can't have my time again, I've done the next best thing. I volunteered with Time to Change on a project working with mental health trusts to tackle this matter head on, with honesty but also compassion. We have identified ways in which all trusts can improve the experience of those using mental health services. Because, as we say in the project, there is no them or us. Only we. You can read more about it at the end of Chapter 6.

Dementia

I find myself needing to quote from the Bible at this point. In *the New International Version of the New Testament*, Mark Chapter 6, Verse 4 it says:

'And Jesus said to them, "A prophet is not without honour, except in his own town and among his relatives and in his own household."'

I am in no way likening myself to a prophet. But not being accepted or praised locally for the good work for which we are nationally renowned is a common experience for leaders and others who are trying to bring about change. We may receive accolades and support from those in far-off places, while those closer to home ignore us, disbelieve or even belittle us when we try to speak the truth about a wonderful opportunity or something that needs to change. With the benefit of hindsight, this was how it felt for me when I began speaking to my colleagues in the local NHS about the impact of dementia on our collective health and care system and how we needed to work together or risk all of our services becoming overwhelmed.

I recall a meeting in 2004 when my attempts to raise the subject were described, albeit politely, as irrelevant and exaggerated by colleagues running primary care, acute and ambulance trusts. In 2007, at a meeting with local partners, considerable animosity was expressed by commissioners about a proposal I made to develop and implement a shared dementia strategy. This was despite us collectively serving the oldest population in the country, and one in which we already knew that people with dementia were being extremely poorly served by the NHS and social care system.

I didn't give up. And by 2009, I was tasked by the SHA to lead this work. There was still considerable denial about the scale of the problem facing us all, and anger directed at me and my organisation, because I had raised the issue in the first place and refused to stop raising it. Commissioners were under pressure to save money from NHS mental health services, and the thought of new investment in dementia care terrified them.

By this time, I had started sharing a vision that we had a collective responsibility, given the size of our population of older people, to make Sussex the best place to receive dementia care and also to become a centre of dementia research excellence.

Commissioners disagreed. They held a counter belief, borne out of a misunderstanding about the financial regime governing foundation trusts, that Sussex Partnership was somehow sitting on a massive financial underspend that ought by rights to be given back to them. The legally binding nature of the requirement of our regulator, Monitor, to return a 6 per cent surplus (a relatively tiny margin compared with most organisations of our size outside the NHS) was not understood. And I think there were one or two who may have deliberately chosen to believe we had more slack available than we really did because it suited the unpleasant purpose they had been allocated, which was to extract as many savings as possible from mental health services and return them for spending in other parts of the NHS.

This is, after all, how mental health services have been treated in the South East and many other parts of England for at least 50 years, and why investment has been so poor and innovation has lagged in all areas, not only dementia. But I mention it here because improving care for people with dementia is of such great importance for the whole NHS. And where Sussex, with its very high elderly population, should be leading the way.

There was also considerable work to do within our own services. With a handful of notable exceptions, neither our clinical nor our managerial staff saw the compelling need for change. Or if they did, they were too overwhelmed by the enormity of the task to try. Status quo was much less challenging, despite increasing levels of unmet need.

In spite of this collective opposition, in February 2010 we launched our trust document *Towards a Sussex Dementia Strategy*, and invited Professor Sube Banerjee, then national Clinical Director for Dementia, to speak at our launch event.

Sube's views on things at the time were:

- It was cruel and unfair that the majority of people experiencing dementia had no diagnosis plus no specific treatment or management plan
- That dementia research was in its infancy and needed a massive boost in attention and investment
- That the NHS and social care system was currently unfit to respond to the needs of people with dementia
- And that if we didn't all sort ourselves out, the whole health and care system in the UK faced a dementia tsunami that could otherwise engulf services

And he has been proven right.

Sube's presentation helped persuade a small group of clinical and managerial colleagues to agree that something had to change. We were determined to improve the experience for people in Sussex with dementia. Somehow, we persuaded commissioners to use short term savings to invest in dementia in-reach teams for those care homes that most frequently sent people to Accident and Emergency Departments for no good reason; the evidence suggests that for anything other than fractures, other major trauma or serious medical incident, people with dementia fare much better if they can remain in familiar surroundings. We also invested in dementia crisis services to help people stay in their own homes, and moved from old age mental health services for all conditions to more specialised services for those with dementia.

There will be those reading this who will say that this decision caused detriment to services for older people with depression and other functional mental illnesses. And I don't doubt they are right. To do the job properly, we would have needed significant new investment because of the increase in demand. And this wasn't forthcoming. However, we did move from a position of less than 40 per cent of people with some form of dementia getting seen, diagnosed and offered ongoing support, to over 75 per cent in only a few years. That is a tangible improvement. The support we gave to people with dementia and their families wasn't as much or as good as I would have liked it to have been in every case, and we dealt with some very distressing complaints. But I also heard how excellent the care was in many cases, and in particular how caring and compassionate the staff were not only towards people affected by dementia, but also to those who loved them and looked after them.

Anyway, we stuck with it. It helped to have a supportive chair and board, and good relationships with both Brighton and Sussex Medical School and the University of Sussex. We agreed to jointly fund a professorial position. After two years of careful preparation, in July 2012 we were able to announce that Professor Sube

Banerjee would be joining us later that year as our first joint Professor of Dementia.

Sube gave his inaugural lecture on 27 February 2014 entitled *Dementia: Reasons to be Cheerful*. It was a tour de force. And it was my honour to give the vote of thanks. If you can, do watch the lecture on YouTube[17]. In it, Sube explains why there are so many people who feel unhappy that we are diagnosing more people with dementia. Dementia carries a great deal of stigma, and it makes many people uncomfortable. It is where cancer used to be, a disease that people feel ashamed of and embarrassed about. And that has got to change, given the prevalence and the cruelty of maintaining that position. And there really are already reasons to be cheerful about dementia.

Sube is now Associate Dean at Brighton and Sussex Medical School as well as Director of the Centre for Dementia Studies. I am extremely grateful to him for joining us in Sussex. He has undoubtedly been a game-changer.

So, too, have some others who had been around for a while longer. I finish this section by offering my profound thanks to Naji Tabet, Mandy Assin, Neil Waterhouse, Moktar Isaac, Gosia Racjek and many, many others who work with people with dementia. Thank you for joining me on that improvement journey and for your continued support to patients and carers who others sometimes shy away from or consider to be too difficult or demanding to help.

And finally, I will make a special mention of a senior nurse I started working with in 2001 and who sadly passed away aged only 57 in 2012. Colin Lindridge was one of the nicest people I have ever known. His kindness, his wisdom and his love for his colleagues and for people with dementia shone like a blazing light. His memory lives on through the good work people do at the Lindridge Centre, named in his honour.

---

[17] www.youtube.com/watch?v=iWu_wBPDDBQ

Returning to my quote at the beginning, and directly addressing people who care for those who have dementia, and help their families: you are prophets and also angels. People like you persuaded me that dementia was serious and something to which we needed to pay proper attention. Our work is beginning to make a real difference. I'm truly proud to have worked with you all.

Research

Writing about research into dementia brings me to research more generally. Like all the stories in this chapter, my experience of supporting the development of research was by no means an unmitigated success. But overall, what we achieved together was considerable.

One of the main reasons for setting up Sussex Partnership from the three smaller trusts was because we wanted our academic partners at Brighton and Sussex Medical School, The University of Sussex and Brighton University to take notice of us and understand the contribution we could make. We did not want to be junior NHS partners who were treated politely but whose views and potential contributions were not seriously considered. We also wanted to avoid a situation in which getting research of any magnitude underway meant reaching agreements about priorities with so many decision makers that serious researchers would give up making the effort.

And I wanted to put mental health services in Sussex on the map for the right reasons, rather than remaining forever in what was effectively the Third Division for mental health care, with limited resources, nothing special to commend us, and the associated challenges about recruiting and retaining good people. The best clinical staff are attracted to places where teaching takes place and where colleagues ask interesting questions and are active researchers as well as implementers of international, peer reviewed research findings.

All of this leads to patients getting better care, which should be our number one goal.

After the merger in 2006, we appointed a new team of executive directors. Dr Kay Macdonald, who had recently joined the trust in West Sussex as Director of Therapies, agreed to take the lead in Research and Development. We already had one Professor, the brilliant Hugo Critchley, who at the time was exploring Tourette's Syndrome and associated conditions, and is currently engaged in internationally important research into consciousness at the University of Sussex Sackler Centre for Consciousness Science, of which he is a co-founder. Kay persuaded me that we needed a Director of Research and Development who was not only an able researcher themselves, but would also have time to devote to building a department. We appointed our Director, Dr Mark Hayward, later that same year.

Mark and I came to an early agreement. There were little pockets of research tucked away within the services that came together to form Sussex Partnership. Some of these were useful, and a handful of people such as Hugo were engaged in world-class studies. But some were of questionable value, and I remember someone, possibly me, calling this kind of research Mickey Mouse. That became our slogan; no Mickey Mouse research.

It was hard in the early days; we didn't want to pull the plug on anyone unfairly. But equally we did not have the resources to support myriad tiny projects, and we did not want to support research that was not of good quality. Mark had a series of polite but difficult conversations with people to explain that the trust could no longer support research which stood little chance of being published in high quality, peer-reviewed journals. We also had to stop some clinical trials which benefitted those administering them more than the collective good. And we needed to amass a team of researchers who were not in all cases the usual suspects.

At the same time, there were some hidden gems. Dr Naji Tabet, who I mentioned earlier in relation to dementia, had been beavering away as part of a national programme of research known as DENDRON (which as well as being a structure in neurology stands for Dementias and Neurodegeneration Network). Naji was a much better example of a prophet who had previously not been known in his own country than me. But Mark changed that, and Naji's work became a driving reason for dementia to become one of the trust's main research groups.

There was also good work into psychosis under Dr Kathy Greenwood, and the bare bones of a strategy for placing people who used our services at the centre of planning for all our research projects. This was considerably enhanced when Ruth Chandler joined us and set up the Lived Experience Advisory Forum (LEAF), which by the time I left had grown to have over 100 members.

In 2008, we held our first small research conference at the University of Sussex. Mark's initial team of seven researchers had grown by then to 15 members. The conference was attended by John Bacon CB, our then new chair. John had worked closely with teaching hospitals throughout his NHS career. He knew that research was key to changing health care for the better, and he challenged us to be much more ambitious with our strategy and to grow our research income from a few hundred thousand pounds per annum to over a million.

The following year, we had a visit from Professor (now Dame) Sally Davies, who became Chief Medical Officer and these days wakes me in the mornings admonishing John Humprys on BBC Radio Four *Today* about alcohol consumption. Sally was at the time NHS Director of Research and Development. During her visit, she was her usual forthright self, and gave us some invaluable tips. The one I remember most was about not trying to do a bit of everything, but rather to specialise unashamedly and to build from strength. We followed her advice over subsequent years, holding research conferences every June which grew better and more ambitious as the team grew in confidence and experience. And in 2013, Sussex Partnership was awarded the prestigious *Health Service Journal* Clinical Research Impact award for going above and beyond in embedding research into everyday practice and patient experience. I am pretty certain it was the members of the LEAF who wowed the judges when they interviewed the shortlisted trusts. As so often they wowed me.

In June 2014, I attended my final Sussex Partnership Research and Development conference. The R and D team by now numbered over 70, mainly clinicians who enhanced their clinical practice by being active researchers. These included Professor Sube Banerjee who I have already mentioned, and our newest recruit, Professor David Fowler, a national expert in anxiety and depression in young people. In the one year we worked together, I learned much from David that I would have found helpful when I was an anxious and troubled teenager myself, but which I can still use to good effect now. Among the 70 members of that team are a handful of dedicated administrative and technical staff. The Sussex Education Centre where they are all based is one of the friendliest, most purposeful workplaces I have ever visited.

Just one final word about Mindfulness, a calming and centreing technique that is used by many of us, but which Dr Mark Hayward and brilliant colleagues such as Dr Clara Strauss continue to explore with people with serious mental illnesses where psychosis and in particular, disturbance by intrusive voices are significant features. I treasure their book, *Overcoming Distressing Voices*[18] which was originally published in 2009. Mental health care is about so much more than medication.

---

[18] https://www.cambridge.org/core/journals/bjpsych-bulletin/article/overcoming-distressing-voices-a-selfhelp-guide-using-cognitive-behavioral-techniques-mark-hayward-clara-strauss-david-kingdon-constable-robinson-2012

And I feel honoured to have played my very small part in helping to build a body of knowledge that is helping people not just in Sussex, but across the UK and the world. Do take a look at the Sussex Mindfulness Centre [19]; they are doing ground breaking work. I feel very proud to have been associated with it.

Better by Experience

I've mentioned in the previous chapter how, after becoming a foundation trust, we got a little over-enthusiastic about becoming more businesslike, at the expense of what was more natural to our culture and values. We turned this around using two sister strategies called Better by Design and Better by Experience. It brings me great satisfaction to be able to say more about Better by Experience here.

Having allowed foundation trust status to go a little to our heads, we felt we needed to do some work to refresh our values. We did this by asking two members of the executive team, Sue Morris and Vincent Badu, to work with me and others in the team; plus a number of our most senior managers, 300 clinical and support staff and some of our patient groups. We were helped by Tim Keogh, a consultant from April Strategies, who along with his colleagues earned every single penny of their very modest fee. I cannot praise them highly enough.

The process can be more valuable than the outcomes in these cases. But this was different.

The output became known as Better by Experience. It was published in lovely little handbooks which we gave to every member of staff, and shared via posters and our intranet. I never have to look up the five commitments of Better by Experience, they are written on my heart. I have listed them here, along with my personal interpretation of what each one means.

---

[19] www.sussexpartnership.nhs.uk/mindfulness

Better by Experience

We welcome you: first impressions really matter, whether you are a patient or a member of staff. We expect everyone to play their part in welcoming people and making them feel comfortable.

We hear you: this is about listening really carefully, especially to people who may appear angry or confused, or who are unable to express themselves. And to each other.

We are helpful: mental health and related services can seem extremely confusing and the routes to get help can be less than straightforward. This commitment is about helping patients in any way possible to get the help they need. And it is about helping and supporting colleagues in work that can be challenging and exhausting.

We work with you: this means sticking with people who may sometimes be extremely difficult to help and even turn it down when it is in their best interests to accept it. It means sticking with people when they do things that disrupt their treatment or are otherwise detrimental to their health. And it means never giving up on anyone.

We are hopeful: for me, this is the most important commitment of all. People who experience mental illness, misuse substances and/or have a learning disability, come across stigma everywhere they go, including within the services that are supposed to help them. They need staff to be hopeful on their behalf so that they can work together to achieve their greatest potential.

We used Better by Experience in recruitment, induction, training and for our staff achievement awards. It was the basis of our revised supervision policy. Looking back through my weekly messages, it featured in over 50 per cent of them. And it was the basis of my leaving speech.

I cannot pretend that it was an unmitigated success, though. Not everyone bought into Better by Experience. Even towards the end of my time at the trust, four years after we had implemented it, I would meet staff who seemed to have no knowledge of these values or who expressed doubt about their relevance or importance in their service. And I think that is because, like name badges, some of our managers didn't own this work themselves or see it as important enough to spend precious time on.

Ultimately that was my fault.

However, despite that, I am still immensely proud of what we did in creating Better by Experience. The most successful organisations place values above strategy in order of importance.

So, if I had my time again, what would I do differently on this subject? Nothing really. I would just do much, much more of it.

My team

There are many things I made mistakes over during my 13 years of running mental health services. They appear throughout this book. I would have needed at least another two volumes to cover them all, but you'll be pleased I resisted!

One area where I felt I got things right more often than not was in the selection and development of a team of people to work with me.

I remember the weeks leading up to my interview on 20 December 2001, when I got my first chief executive role. A lot of pressure was being exerted by senior NHS colleagues to appoint people who were already in the system to avoid redundancy costs. And I took their point; the NHS cannot afford to waste talent, experience or money. This happens all too often in reorganisations.

At the same time, I had been appointed to lead a new organisation with fresh ideas and a more positive, compassionate and less paternalistic attitude towards helping those who from time to time experience mental illness, have a learning disability or misuse substances.

I decided that the senior team who were appointed to lead and run these services needed to be the best and the most diverse they could be. And I said so.

Having got the chief executive job myself, to my delight, my first two appointments, made in January 2002, stood the test of time. At the time of writing, Helen Greatorex is in her second year as chief executive at Kent and Medway Partnership NHS Trust. Helen is an original thinker, not afraid to raise concerns, always has patient wellbeing at the centre of her thinking, and at the same time manages to be a loyal and very funny colleague. Any team would be enhanced by her membership.

And although he decided to try his hand in the acute sector the year after we became a foundation trust, for seven years Spencer Prosser was a brilliant, effective, honourable and courageous finance director. I loved working alongside him.

All the jobs in an executive team are important, but the directors of nursing and finance have always been, for me, the governance lynchpins of the team. So, it was wonderful to find Sally Flint who became my second and final finance director; Sally is a determined and honourable leader, and has now completed 8 years in that job.

When I was off work with a sickly gallbladder in 2011 and again with depression in 2013, Sue Morris, by then Executive Director of Corporate Services, was the obvious choice to be asked by the chair to step in as Acting chief executive. As my chair John Bacon used to say, every organisation needs a Sue. We first met in September

2002, and she joined the team in January 2003. Sue helped me understand how much I had missed by not having completed general management training. She tackled any project with thoroughness and skill. She is also the most positive person I have ever worked with; every meeting I had with her was a joy.

All leaders make appointments that don't work out; this happened to me too, but I'm not going to mention anyone in this regard. I take more than the lion's share of responsibility when the fit was not right. I was given a great bit of advice early on from Duncan Selbie, who now runs Public Health England, but in my early chief executive days acted as a mentor to me. He said that, in parting company with someone, others will be watching. So be kind, treat the person who is leaving really well, and do everything you can to enable them to go with dignity. On the few times I have needed to do this, I always tried to heed those words. If it didn't seem that way to anyone reading this, I am truly sorry. I would still commend anyone who might need it to listen to that advice.

Medical directors came and went more often than other team members in my time as a chief executive. It is hard to find doctors who are prepared to set the clinical practice they have trained for to one side and do the hard yards as an executive team member. But in April 2010, in an interview that I will describe in a later chapter, I found someone who had the potential to do a truly great job. Dr Tim Ojo is an excellent psychiatrist and a thoroughly good man. It was an honour to work with him for four years. He helped me personally more than anyone but he will ever know.

Great clinicians do not always make good leaders, but the opposite is the case for two others in my team. Lorraine Reid and Dr Kay Macdonald are respectively a senior nurse and a psychologist who were at the top of their professions when they moved into management. Both brought intelligence, vision and kindness to our shared enterprise.

I have mentioned Vincent Badu already in relation to Equality and Human Rights and Better by Experience. Vincent was appointed to lead on social care when we formed Sussex Partnership in 2006. I used to call him my secret weapon. His exceptional interpersonal skills, emotional intelligence and beatific smile could warm the frostiest atmosphere.

The newest member to join the team was Sam Allen. I first met Sam in 2001 when she was a commissioner. I think we always knew we would work together one day. She was already a senior manager at Sussex Partnership in 2013 when I carried out a mini-restructure and created a space that Sam was more than able to fill within the executive team. Sam became chief executive at Sussex Partnership in 2017.

That restructure was partly driven by the retirement of Ann Merricks, who from 2005 – 2013 helped me and the board to merge, become a foundation and teaching trust and to stay on top of a myriad of projects and governance issues. Ann is the opposite of me, always calm and never excitable. I loved knowing she was in the office next door. For her, it was more of a mixed blessing!

I would also like to thank Kevin O'Shea, Mark Heathcote, Andrew Partington, Neil Perkins, Andrew Kelly, Kim Shamash, Fiona Whiting and Anna Lewis who for shorter periods were members of the team. They were all a pleasure to work with.

I wasn't always the easiest of bosses. At times, I didn't respond well to stress. I was very good at starting things and rather less good at seeing them through. I could wear people out with new ideas and initiatives.

And I didn't like it when members of the team disagreed with one another. Like an over-anxious parent, I wanted the children to get along nicely. But I had to learn that I wasn't their mother and they weren't my children. Healthy debate is important, especially as we were wrestling with questions for which there were no easy answers. They told me this, and I tried really hard not only to listen, but also to change.

What kept us together, and made the whole greater than the sum of the parts, was that I somehow managed to find people who shared the same values, about equality and fairness and only competing for contracts where we knew we could make a difference, and wanting above all else, to make a difference for people who had often been dealt the roughest of hands.

For the most part, I think we achieved that together.

Chapter 10

The more horrid parts of the job

Introduction

There are some sections of this book that I dreaded writing but I knew had to be faced. A few were so painful that I found myself giving up for a while. When I eventually forced myself back to my writing table, I made myself do it in very small chunks interspersed with distraction activities. At one point I came very close to jettisoning the whole project, despite having by then completed three quarters of it. I'm glad I wrote about how I was feeling at the time, otherwise I would have completely forgotten those negative thoughts. Because despite the grimmer moments, writing the book and facing the feelings it evoked has been a really important part of how I have moved on into my new world.

Although I am writing about the things in the job I didn't like, it feels good to be able to get them off my chest and share them with you in the hope they may be of help.

Some of the points will be obvious, especially to those that know me well. But others may surprise even them.

One of my ways of coping is to pretend to be feeling completely wonderful when I'm not. I have learned through therapy that this comes at a personal cost to me, but is also annoyingly Pollyanna-ish to those who work with me, AND to my family and friends.

Since my last significant episode of depression, I've been learning to recalibrate and set my dials to include some more midrange responses to enquiries on how I'm doing, using words like '**OK**' and '**fine**', rather than '**amazing**' or '**brilliant**'. And I've noticed people noticing the change in me. I'm not completely sure what they think of the new me, but I guess that's their issue and not mine.

So I offer this chapter in my recently-learned spirit of honesty and less manufactured positivity.

Accreditations, audits and inspections

One of the reasons I would pretend to myself that everything was wonderful even when it wasn't, is because I really don't like complaining. I'm not very keen on it in others, but more than anything I dislike it in myself. I believe that people who seem to derive satisfaction from finding fault can be very bad for our collective wellbeing. They drag others down, including me.

Perhaps it is because such people trigger fears in me that I am at risk of being found out to be a charlatan? They make me feel guilty, even when I know deep down that I have nothing to hide. I don't want to have that impact on anyone else. But of course, a leader who never finds fault would be pretty useless.

My reaction to criticism almost certainly taps into feelings of inadequacy from my younger, less happy years. I can think of examples from different points in my earlier life - a joyless colleague when I first qualified as a health visitor who always seemed to be trying to catch me out and was clearly triumphant when she did, and a nurse tutor who seemed to be able to look into my soul and predict I would never come to any good. There have been other, more recent, examples but it is probably best I don't name them.

I am not in any way saying that everyone whose job it is to question, probe or pass judgement falls into this category. I have met wonderful inspectors, regulators, commissioners, members of select committees and other panels who seem to be able to ask searching questions openly and to give constructive and supportive feedback even when their main role is to look for faults.

Someone who epitomises compassion while never compromising her values is Andrea Sutcliffe, Director of Social Care at the Care Quality Commission (CQC). She is one of those top managers who will always be her own woman. I love that she turns up to meetings in her colourful baseball shoes carrying a small canvas rucksack. Social care, which includes nursing homes, is a far better place because of Andrea. Her Twitter name is @CrouchEndTiger7. She really is a small tiger with a heart of gold.

I greatly respect people who can do these jobs well because I know I would make a poor auditor or CQC inspector myself. I've made an art form out of accentuating the positive, less so regarding negative stuff. I have done a great deal of work improving how I give constructive feedback through learning to become a coach. People say I do it well. But when I was a chief executive and responsible for everything, I didn't like myself when I had to be incisive and critical. It brought out the worst in me. The overwhelming sense of responsibility made me anxious and could lead to me being heavy-handed at times.

As this is confession time, I have more to share. When I was a chief executive, I used to dread inspections. When you run a trust with a range of services across a lot of sites, these visits and other such events will occur fairly frequently. I have lost count of the number of times I was interrupted in whatever I was doing to be told that we were having yet another unannounced inspection. My heart would immediately start beating faster. The hard work I put in to hide my anxiety might have sometimes been successful, but it came at a cost, to me and sometimes to others too.

If such occasions made me distracted and uneasy, I cannot imagine how it must have felt for the clinical staff, no matter how many times they had thought about such visits, or practised with colleagues from other parts of the trust on what to do in order to give of their best when an inspector called.

To those colleagues who ever saw me showing signs of fraying, or who did not feel as supported as they should have when an inspection or audit produced a result that was surprising, and not in a nice way, I offer my heartfelt apologies. And to those who probably thought of me up in my chief executive ivory tower being totally unaffected by the things that scared them, I apologise too. Perhaps if they had known how I felt, it might have made things easier for them?

Investigations by any of the 50 or so bodies who in their various ways hold chief executives and other trust board members to account feel to me far too much like a lottery. And this is not right. Although the criteria used are intended to be standardised and available for all to know and understand, the interpretation can vary widely. This is how it can come to pass that a service that gets the highest possible score via one well regarded national accreditation scheme can be found seriously wanting the following year by a different set of inspectors. Such variation leaves staff confused and senior managers struggling to explain what has happened to patients, families and other interested parties, as well as losing confidence in their own judgement.

If I could have one wish for the NHS regarding inspection, it would be this. There should be a great deal less of it. And what there is should be of a much higher and more meaningful quality. The whole of the NHS would benefit from investment in information systems that provide incontrovertible evidence about the quality and outcomes of care, so that these can be interpreted in the same way by providers, commissioners, professional and service regulators. Politicians, who understandably want to get re-elected, would then perhaps stop being able to act like agents of the *Daily Mail*, handpicking partial bits of NHS data and using them to overstate or misrepresent a situation in order to meet their political ends.

Because what happens in the NHS is far more important than that.

Lack of privacy

For an extrovert like me, being spotted browsing in Marks and Spencer on a Saturday should be no big deal. But at the end of a bad week, the longing to be anonymous can be considerable. I think of that iconic photograph of Cherie Blair on the day after Labour won the election in 1997. She opened her front door to take in the milk and was caught unawares in her nightie by paparazzi. I've no pretensions that I am in her league in terms of media interest, but during my time as an NHS chief executive, public servants in leadership roles became increasingly fair game for the media.

Over the winter of 2015/16, two extremely honourable NHS chief executives, one of whom was retiring and the other who had agreed to take on running an additional trust considerably less successful than their own, both received a media monstering over their salaries. In the case of the retiring CE, the media simply got the figures wrong and confused the accrued pension entitlement with a massive pay-off, which this person had neither asked for nor received. I feel so angry for the person concerned, who is one of the most thoughtful, compassionate and honourable people I know, because no correction was made. And even if it had been, there will still be people who believe they got massive amounts of public money that they didn't deserve.

In the case of the second CE, they effectively took on a new job, merging their trust which was known for outstanding results, with one that was considered to be failing, thus placing their considerable track record of success at risk for the greater good of the patients and staff concerned. The new board felt this warranted a modest pay uplift, which they defended. But it was the chief executive's face that got splashed across the media. They have had to meet people in the street who have read and believed them to be an uncaring fat cat, depriving nurses of a pay rise, according to one headline, even though nurses' pay is set nationally and the new increased salary was still less than a middle manager in a bank would receive, without bonuses.

I had my fair share of difficult media during my 13 years as a chief executive, sometimes about mistakes that were made in the very complex cases we looked after. One particular example concerned an in-depth survey we carried out into why some of our staff were consistently telling us via the national staff survey that they didn't feel supported in their work. The staff who took part in the more detailed survey were a relatively small group of 300 or so. With hindsight, they were not representative. Also, some of the questions were purposefully loaded to test thoughts and feelings on the challenging topic of bullying at work. I know some of our managers felt that the findings were overstated and not statistically significant.

Nonetheless, I and all of the board took the results extremely seriously because our staff had taken part. And we published them. Apart from anything else, not doing so would have looked like a cover-up. But it was badly misreported. The headlines about allegations of traits of a bullying and blame culture still haunt me. All this happened at a time when I wasn't at my best. In fact, I learned of the findings on coming back to work after being off sick with depression myself.

But this is what we get paid for as leaders. It goes with the territory. If you can't cope with being commented on as you pick up some groceries or can't bear the thought of appearing on the front page of the local paper in a negative story, I guess you shouldn't do the job.

I will just mention one important paradox. There is a particular sort of leader who truly doesn't care what other people think about them. And they are those people who are sometimes labelled as psychopaths or sociopaths. There is some useful literature on this. Jon Ronson's book *The Psychopath Test*[20] is fascinating and takes many twists and turns. A 2013 article in Forbes called *The Disturbing Link between Psychopathy and Leadership*[21] is perhaps more accessible. It relates directly to the subject of psychopathic tendencies among those in senior positions, suggesting that the

---

[20] The Psychopath Test, Jon Ronson, Picador 2011

[21] http://www.forbes.com/sites/victorlipman/2013/04/25/the-disturbing-link-between-psychopathy-and-leadership/

estimate elsewhere of 3 per cent of senior leaders being psychopaths is overstated. Which is a relief.

But we do need to be careful. If we treat public sector leaders so badly that only those who are psychopaths apply, that percentage could increase.

And that would be very bad for all of us.

Having your motives misinterpreted and things made up about you

Many of us have a tendency to think that our own motives are unassailable, but at the same time question the motivations of others, particularly those in the public eye. Attribution theory offers explanations on why this happens.

In *Simply Psychology*[22], Sam Mcleod sets out the differences between how we assign causes of behaviour to others and to ourselves, as originally described by Heider in 1958.

1. Internal Attribution: The process of assigning the cause of behaviour to some internal characteristic, rather than to outside forces. When we explain the behaviour of others we look for enduring internal attributions, such as personality traits. For example, we attribute the behaviour of a person to their personality, motives or beliefs.

2. External Attribution: The process of assigning the cause of behaviour to some situation or event outside a person's control rather than to some internal characteristic. When we try to explain our own behaviour we tend to make external attributions, such as situational or environment features.

Knowing this helps a little, but it doesn't completely take away the pain of having your motives questioned or even, as it may sometimes feel, deliberately misinterpreted. For someone like me

---

[22] http://www.simplypsychology.org/attribution-theory.html

who has a high need for approval, it was one of the hardest aspects of the job.

There is an added aspect that is relevant to my situation. And it will be to yours if you choose mental health. Which is that people who work in mental health services don't, as a rule, crave authority. I've already mentioned this when writing about name badges.

I know there are some who will strongly disagree. Particularly those patients who have been detained under the Mental Health Act or experienced other forcible ways of being made to comply with treatment. They may strongly believe the opposite to be true. They may feel that some of the people who work in mental health like authority rather too much, especially when they are meting it out. And I am sure they have a point. But from my recent work with Time to Change, it seems that those who purposefully abuse their position of power are, thankfully, in a very small minority.

My observation, unproven in any scientific way, is that people who are attracted to work in mental health and related services tend to be: comfortable with ambiguity; like working on their own or in small teams; are highly creative and don't generally appreciate being told what to do. They also tend, and again this is a gross generalisation, to be more left leaning politically than healthcare workers generally, and to view managers and leaders as the mouthpieces and the servants of government. I know this in part because I identify with this view myself.

As a mental health leader who has to implement compliance with policies and procedures, one can thus start out at something of a disadvantage. However hard you try to communicate a more bottom-up, egalitarian approach, there will be a small number of rules that have to be followed and certain things that have to be done.

During my career as a chief executive, I tried not to insist on rules unless we had to have them. And I know that others around me sometimes found this difficult, especially when so much of our regulation in the latter years was based on a compliance regime.

It is important to remember also that however much you try, people will misinterpret things you say and do. Here is a benign example. At my office, I paid for real coffee for myself and made sure we had enough for visitors. People always said they liked it. I thought it was welcoming. But one day, at a meeting elsewhere in the trust, someone apologised for offering me instant coffee and said they knew I didn't approve of people drinking it. I felt quite upset. I had never in my life said such a thing. I was happy to drink instant coffee. But somehow, my action of offering coffee in a cafetiere myself had turned into a folklore that I disapproved of anyone who didn't drink real coffee.

As I say, this is a benign example. I can think of worse.

As a leader, all you can do to counteract such misinterpretations is to be yourself, surround yourself with people who are also genuine and show what your beliefs and values are through your actions as well as your words.

No time to think

There are many paradoxes to being a leader in a public service as closely scrutinised as the NHS. One of these is that, in a job where the main tool of the trade is one's intellect, there is often quite literally no time to think.

There are a number of reasons for this. Firstly, for good and not-so-good reasons, everyone wants to have a piece of you. If you don't attend this or that event, staff, governors, partners, patient representatives, even members of the public, may see it as a slight, a sign that you don't view the thing they are meeting about as important. There is a tendency to overfill the diary and to try to get to as many events as possible. When I was a chief executive, my schedule felt punishing by my own standards. But then I would talk to others and find that some were starting their days even earlier than I was, going to even more events and finishing even later.

Secondly, emails and post. Emails have not completely taken over the post, but we are getting close. At least post only needs to be dealt with once a day. In the chapter on communications, I said that when I started in 2001, I would get about 50 emails a day, and by the time I left in 2014, I was receiving around 200.

Reading these emails and deciding what to do with them is in itself a fulltime job. The number that genuinely need the attention of the chief executive are undoubtedly a small proportion of that number, but the worry is that, unless they all receive careful attention, something really critical will be missed.

I believed strongly that if a person had taken the trouble to write to me with concerns about the care being provided, I, or someone whose judgement and objectivity I trusted absolutely, should read their letter or email, then make every effort to be satisfied that the investigation and response were robust as well as sensitive. There is no such thing as a simple complaint in mental health and related services. We used a grading system, but despite lots of checks and balances, I was always worried that something I would consider really serious would somehow slip through the net. And sometimes it did. All in all, I would say that about a day a week on average was taken up with issues relating to patient concerns. Given that we were caring for 50,000 patients per year, this does not seem unreasonable, but it might surprise some people.

Then there are the external demands on one's time. Accountability is an overused term, as is governance. Both these words and their derivatives can be used by organisations external to providers of NHS care in sometimes punitive ways. If every demand for the chief executive to see, understand and act on a piece of information or guidance were to be adhered to, there would be no time at all left to run the trust.

And that is when things are going well. My heart goes out to those running trusts in 'special measures' (or whatever the latest term is by the time this book comes out). The torrent of attention such organisations receive can feel very much less than helpful, and is almost always a distraction from the real work that needs to be done.

Finally, as Harold Macmillan is reported to have said, there are 'events, dear boy'. No-one could make up the bizarre and occasionally terrible things that come along to throw you off course. They can range from a legionella outbreak that threatens to close down one of your main sites, to a member of staff who has done something harmful either by accident or on purpose - in this case, you almost certainly won't know which for some time but you will be required to comment instantly and avoid sounding wishy-washy if you don't want to get pilloried by the media. Or a patient has harmed themselves or someone else. Or a coach has crashed right outside your building causing major road delays and leaving you with 100 walking wounded to care for. This latter actually happened on the morning of a meeting I shouldn't have missed.

Those who work in emergency planning will say that you should plan for these surprise eventualities. This works up to a point. Whenever such an event happened, I always found it was necessary to take stock of the circumstances, and in particular, assure myself that the people who needed to know things were told in the right way, and that the people who needed to be comforted were being attended to, also in the right way. It can take a lot of time to do this well. According to McKinsey[23], the chief executive and board should spend 60 per cent of their time on strategic matters, and 40 per cent on governance. But any NHS chief executive who actually did that in today's world would be lucky to survive their first year. I

23

http://www.mckinsey.com/insights/strategy/tapping_the_strategic_pot ential_of_boards notice that several have lost their jobs in the past year for failing to have enough grip on operational issues.

When things go wrong for NHS leaders, it seems to me that the unravelling can start because the actions taken at the outset haven't been sufficient to address the concerns of the interested parties. My blog, reproduced at the end of this section, proved popular with NHS leaders when I posted it in December 2015. It includes some advice about what to do when something goes wrong. I hope it will prove helpful if you haven't previously seen it.

Some chief executives go to conferences to get away from the office and find time to think. I have done that on occasions, but it didn't really work for me. There were too many people and things to distract me. I needed quiet, and that was really hard to come by.

My advice is the same as advice about anything difficult that you face. There is no rule book on how to do these jobs and therefore no right answers on how much time you should spend on this or that. You have to decide.

But I will just say this. If you allow yourself to be consumed by meetings, operational issues and other people's agendas, as I occasionally did, you definitely won't have time to think. And you probably won't do your job as well as you might. I needed silence and space, and just a few trusted people available to bounce ideas off, and then more time and more quiet. It took me a long time to learn that if I rush, I make the wrong decision.

Only you know what you need. And you owe it to yourself, the patients you serve and the staff you lead to make sure you get it.

The hardest thing of all

I've been watching the desperately sad story unfold of the awful, untimely, preventable death of a young man with learning disabilities. Only those most closely involved can comment on what led to his death. But what happened afterwards has become extremely public.

Having done the job I once did, I feel the need to share some thoughts. I know this may provoke strong reactions. But to be silent suggests complicity about unfair discrimination of vulnerable people, lack of compassion and the opposite of openness in how the NHS too often deals with mistakes. And I am not complicit.

The media, including social media, can be a massive force for good. The media can shed light on things that need to be uncovered, especially where the interested parties are far apart. And in the case of campaigning journalists like Shaun Lintern, they can help families eventually get to the truth. Although they really shouldn't have to.

The NHS is at long last waking up to the fact that the public understand bad things can happen. The public know that the NHS is staffed by humans who, by dint of being human, make mistakes. And that there are risks inherent in almost everything that the NHS does or doesn't do. They know some mistakes occur because staff are careless or stressed or tired or overstretched or poorly trained or badly led. And they are realistic; they also know that a small number of staff do terrible things deliberately. But the NHS still needs to appreciate that the public will not accept cover ups.

Below are some of my lessons on running services for vulnerable people, learned the hard way, by experience. And by not getting things right myself all of the time.

1. Running NHS services is very, very hard. The hardest part is when things go wrong and patients are harmed or die in circumstances where this could have been

The hardest thing of all (Cont)

prevented. It is what causes those in senior positions, like the one I once held, sleepless nights and to question our own fitness to lead. If leaders don't have sleepless nights like this, they are almost certainly in the wrong job. Being a decent leader in one of these very hard jobs starts with having respect and compassion for those we serve. And the humility to admit mistakes.

2. *Leaders in the NHS need to be curious and ask questions. They need to seek the truth, however hard this may be. They should surround themselves with others who are curious too and not afraid to challenge their leader. They need clinicians of the highest integrity with deep knowledge of the care they are responsible for to advise them. And although non-executive directors and governors who pose difficult questions may occasionally be wearisome, good leaders know that such people are invaluable at questioning what might seem obvious and to upholding core values. I may not always have shown this, but it is what I truly believe.*

3. *Some time after I left, I noticed that my old trust had been criticised for apparently taking too long to complete serious incident reviews. And I recalled my own occasional frustration at the length of time it took to receive outcomes from a review when I was desperate for answers. But now I'm thinking again. Investigating something properly takes time, especially when extremely distressed people are involved. Those investigating must be open minded and objective. They need to be released from other duties. They must not take everything they are told at face value. And they need the remit and backing to do whatever is needed to*

get to the facts. *Timeliness is important, but not at the expense of uncovering the truth.*

4. *I recall an attempted homicide by a patient. We were so concerned to find out whether we risked a recurrence that, rather than an internal investigation, we immediately commissioned a specialist independent organisation to investigate and report to us, with no holds barred, on the care and treatment of this patient. This informed us about some changes we needed to make. This approach was later commended by the coroner. But when a statutory independent review was eventually carried out more than three years after the incident, the reviewers devoted space in their report to criticising us for having commissioned that first report, even though they broadly concurred with the findings. There is no rule book for NHS leaders. You must work out what to do yourself. And often only learn with hindsight whether you got a decision right or wrong.*

5. *The media onslaught that can occur after a serious incident can be all consuming and deeply distracting. The worst thing that can happen is that you are diverted from the real job, of providing good care and rooting out any that is less than good, into so-called 'media handling'. I have been very close to getting badly distracted myself on occasions. My saving grace was probably having been a nurse first. But I don't think that being a clinician is by any means essential to being a good NHS leader. Caring about what happens to patients is the only essential qualification.*

6. *Apologising is never easy. But it can mean so much. Apologies should be sincere, whole-hearted, unqualified and platitude-free. They may not be accepted initially. They may have to be repeated, sometimes many times.*

The hardest thing of all (Cont)

The hardest meetings for me and those I worked with during my 13 years as an NHS chief executive were with families whose loved ones had come to harm in our care. But I am so grateful to those people for giving me the opportunity to listen really carefully to them and to apologise to them in person. It may take a long time to achieve such a meeting, and sometimes several are needed. The effort is really worth it.

7. *The NHS is a microcosm of society and is institutionally discriminatory towards those who experience mental illness or have a learning disability. This is manifest in poor staff attitudes, low expectations, inadequate investment, silo thinking, paucity of data including comparative benchmark information on incidents, and the negative way the rest of the NHS treats those who raise concerns about such things. I'm doing my tiny bit as a volunteer to improve matters but there is so much more for all of us to do.*

8. *Talk of 'numbers' without benchmarks and other good quality comparators can also be a distraction. Every unexpected death of a vulnerable person needs to be investigated to see if it could have been prevented. And that takes resources, which are in short supply in mental health services these days where the brunt of cuts have been made despite all the rhetoric about 'parity of esteem'. Coroners are also overwhelmed; it often takes years before inquests into such deaths are completed, which is agony for the families.*

> *It really shouldn't matter whether the person who died was young, talented, beautiful, courageous, funny or anything else. They were a person who mattered. My heart goes out to anyone who has lost a loved one, and especially to those whose deaths were in some way preventable. You have to live with 'if only' for the rest of your lives.*
>
> *And that is the hardest thing of all.*

Being lonely

Until very close to retirement, there was no chance that I would have been able to admit, even to myself, that I found myself feeling lonely at times during my 13 years of being a chief executive. It seems an odd thing to say, as, apart from anything else, I was almost always surrounded by people. As well as the multiple events and meetings one attends as a chief executive, and the constant demand to be with others, I was a member of several teams, including the board, the executive team, our wider trust leadership team and teams I joined with external partners to achieve the greater good for the communities we collectively served.

But in each of these teams, as chief executive you find yourself in a unique position. You are the accountable officer for the organisation, and people look to you to know what to do and to step forward to deal with the most difficult stuff, particularly in the public arena. It is no different for any leader, but there is something peculiar to being a public sector leader these days that makes the position uniquely exposed.

In those wider external teams, you are not really a team in the true sense, even when your agreed purpose is to seek the common good. Individually you are each compromised by having to consider the impact on your own patients and staff of seeking that good. There will always be competition for resources. This is especially so for those leading mental health services; we have learned from all the evidence collected in recent years that they lose out financially to other parts of the NHS at the most challenging of times.

My loneliness was offset by being surrounded by great people, the support of my chair and the rest of the board, and having folk outside I could talk to. I had various coaches and mentors during my 13 years; each was invaluable in their own way. I also used to share thoughts with a small number of other chief executives. And I was in an action learning set for a number of years, which provided a safe place to share challenges and anxieties.

Nonetheless, it was a lonely job. Waking up in the small hours because of a problem one has been wrestling with happens to most of us. What makes the chief executive position different from any other is that heavy weight of accountability that hangs over any decision you arrive at, however many people you involve in coming to that decision.

Most of the time, I relished it. Towards the end, I found it made me frightened and unsure. And the last thing any organisation needs is a leader who is feeling like that. It was time for me to hang up my boots.

Chapter 11

On suicide

I knew a simple soldier boy
Who grinned at life in empty joy,
Slept soundly through the lonesome dark,
And whistled early with the lark.

In winter trenches, cowed and glum,
With crumps and lice and lack of rum,
He put a bullet through his brain.
No one spoke of him again.

You smug-faced crowds with kindling eye
Who cheer when soldier lads march by,
Sneak home and pray you'll never know
The hell where youth and laughter go.

Seigfried Sassoon, Collected War Poems 1918

Introduction

People take their own lives for many reasons – stress, overwhelming debt, fear, loss and loneliness, shame and self-hatred, as well as depression and other mental illnesses. The underlying cause of suicide for most people who contemplate it is lack of hope for the future. The joy of the young soldier in Sassoon's poem, before he encounters the horrors of war, contrasts poignantly with his state of mind as he huddles in terror in a filthy cold trench far from home.

From the poem, we can also see what has become an established research finding: that suicide is more likely when the means to take one's own life are readily available. The young soldier was holding a loaded gun; what might have been a passing thought sadly led to his last act.

Suicide is not only a horrific waste of a life that could have been lived fully and well. It also casts a long, mean shadow on those left behind. In this chapter, I will explore my own changing attitude towards suicide and experiences of it. Not much of this book was easy to write. But this has definitely been the hardest chapter. It is also probably the most important.

Early experiences

I remember a dull-eyed girl at school whose mother died by suicide. She cut a lonely figure, shunned for being different. She occasionally tried to speak about what had happened to her family but was discouraged from doing so by an embarrassed silence from fellow pupils and our teachers. I think of her now, and hope she is alright.

And I recall a jolly boy I used to see in the pub, with whom I and my friends were on nodding terms. One day he was no longer there. Then we read in the local paper that he had poured petrol over himself and set himself alight. There was no funeral service and no way of paying our respects. I still wonder if his poor parents ever came to terms with such a loss.

A few years later, a friend's father took his own life at a time when his family needed him very much. I remember my own father's response which was that it was an extremely selfish thing to have done. He meant well, but he was wrong. I hope I can explain why.

As a student nurse in Cambridge, I looked after people, mostly young women close to my own age, who had self-harmed by taking deliberate overdoses, cutting themselves or swallowing sharp objects. Some were admitted frequently after repeated and similar attempts. The care they were given was peremptory, focussing on counteracting any physical damage. It didn't seem in any way to address the underlying causes of them hurting themselves in the first place.

And I also remember once saying to someone, possibly under the influence of alcohol, that everyone thinks about suicide from time to time. This person looked at me in shock and said no, they didn't.

I'm not so sure. What I do know from those early experiences is that suicide was seen as deeply shameful while I was growing up, and not the sort of thing that happened in nice families or that 'normal' people should ever talk about.

Which is probably why, when I made a botched suicide attempt myself in my early twenties when life just got too hard to bear, that I felt deeply ashamed and didn't tell anyone about it for many years. My shame was compounded by what the nurse who looked after me in A and E said about me being a selfish waste of space and that I had taken him away from looking after other more deserving patients - see the end of Chapter 6. I believed him, and the reason I can remember his words so clearly is because they became embedded in my consciousness and the way I viewed myself for many years.

Shifting attitudes

I don't know whether it is my own experience of depression and occasional thoughts of suicide that lead me to feel so distressed about other people who contemplate it, and even more so about those who actually achieve it. What I do know is that undirected empathy can be exhausting as well as being of no use to those people. It helped me a great deal to feel that I could have some positive impact on the wellbeing of others who sometimes contemplated suicide through my work. But it has also cost me, in sleepless nights and levels of anguish that I mainly hid because I didn't know how to express them.

During the early months of running West Sussex Health and Social Care I felt overwhelmed by incident reports of patients in the community who had taken their own lives. I talked about it with Helen, my wise and knowledgeable Director of Nursing. She tried to explain that a combination of better reporting and a larger area was probably creating the impression that we were at risk of all our patients dying in this way. At my request, she did some further analysis and found that, from the evidence available, our suicide rates at the time were lower than other comparable areas.

But numbers and rates don't matter when you have lost a loved one to suicide. I remember in my very early days as a chief executive meeting the father of a young man with a complex history who had been detained under the Mental Health Act in one of the trust's locked wards. One day, while out walking in the grounds of the hospital accompanied by a member of staff, the young man made a run for it. He had done this before, and would usually be found later at his parents' home not far away. But this time, he made his way to the railway line and lay down on the tracks where he was hit by a fast train. The father brought a framed school photograph of his son to the meeting and set it up on the table facing me. I can recall looking at this lovely boy and trying to control my voice as I said how sorry we were for what had happened. We met a number of times so that I could explain what our investigations had uncovered and some changes we had made in the light of them. I think of that father often; he was a kind and decent man, and helped me to understand the impact of losing someone you love in such an awful way.

I also recall at around the same time having a discussion with a senior psychiatrist. He was expressing considerable anger at what he saw as the latest fad of blaming mental health services after someone had died by suicide. His point was that when a patient eventually dies of cancer, there is no investigation, because the death is expected. Instead, their life is celebrated and the people who have helped them to live longer than might otherwise have been expected are celebrated too. So surely it should be the same for mental health services, and that those who have kept the person alive for so long should receive praise and thanks rather than suspicion and approbation.

I understood why he felt like that. There are some people whose risky behaviour may, it can be argued, almost inevitably lead one day to a fatal event. And there are clearly those for whom the weariness of contemplating yet another negative spiral eventually becomes too much.

But having thought deeply about this subject over a number of years, I find myself disagreeing fundamentally about the inevitability of death by suicide. To accept that such deaths *are* somehow inevitable suggests a hopelessness on behalf of the services that are designed to help people like me, and many reading this, who are troubled by mental illness from time to time. It also flies in the face of the latest research, which shows that if you pay careful attention to a person's suicidal thoughts and ideas, and allow them to express them openly, rather than ignoring them, glossing over them or underplaying their importance, it is likely, although by no means certain, that they will find hope in the interest you are showing, and allow you to work with them to help keep them safe.

This is the basis of the approach taken by Grassroots, the suicide prevention charity of which I was invited to become a trustee when I retired. Grassroots trainers run mental health awareness courses, bespoke programmes like the one we commissioned for the Sussex Partnership executive team in 2013, and the internationally recognised Applied Suicide Intervention Skills Training (ASIST) which I have completed and can highly recommend to anyone. The evidence suggests that, whatever our line of work, we are far more likely to come across someone at risk of suicide than a person who has collapsed because their heart stopped. And yet while millions learn about resuscitation and cardiac massage, relatively few people go on ASIST or equivalent courses. Why so? Because of the stigma of suicide and how uncomfortable talking about it can make us.

Doing the course and being involved with Grassroots has given me much more confidence to ask someone who seems down how they are, and to listen really carefully to their reply. I just wish I had done it sooner.

Woodlands

This chapter would be unfinished if I didn't mention a small cluster of suicides that happened in Sussex in 2009, causing tragedy for the families concerned and even more distress than usual for the staff. I could have included this section in the chapter about things I wish I had done better, but it seems that it really belongs here. All of the details are a matter of public record, because of the high level of media coverage and the subsequent coroner's investigations and reports. But I am sure that the feelings of families will remain raw; I have tried to be as sensitive as possible in what I write.

There were two deaths, both by hanging and both of patients at our smallest hospital, in Hastings. Deaths of people while they are mental hospital inpatients are viewed as the most serious of incidents. And rightly so; mental hospitals should be places of safety, even though for most people, going into hospital is extremely distressing and can actually increase the risk of suicide and self-harm. The tools staff use to mitigate against this are risk assessment; careful and compassionate observation of patients; frequent engagement with each patient; and management of the environment to remove known risks, while doing everything possible to maintain comfort, privacy and dignity. This makes it sound scientific. But no matter how good or careful staff working in these services are, it is impossible to be 100 per cent infallible.

The first death was shocking enough; the person concerned had only been known to our services for a few days, had no previous history of serious mental illness and was a high-profile member of the community. The method used was also previously unknown to any hospital with similar facilities. Because he was being observed frequently, he was found very quickly. But he could not be saved.

The second death, by a different but not altogether dissimilar method, occurred only two months later. It left us reeling. The high profile of the first man who died meant there had already been intense local media coverage. This included criticism of our care from a number of quarters before the facts were known, including getting some of them very wrong. This was exacerbated after the second death, especially when it became clear that we were being investigated by Sussex Police under the possibility of corporate manslaughter, which had only applied to public sector bodies since the previous April. Several deaths that had occurred in previous years at other hospitals were included in the police enquiries, and for a while we felt under siege.

But the hardest part was that the staff at the small hospital in Hastings were experiencing intense local hostility. Even the most senior clinicians had lost confidence in their own ability to keep people safe. For these reasons I and my executive team took perhaps the most difficult decision of our whole careers. We decided to close that hospital with immediate effect, redeploy the staff and carry out a fundamental review.

On the day of the closure, I spent several hours at the hospital. The animosity and distress among the staff was palpable. They felt they were being punished. Nothing I or anyone else said could dissuade them from this. It was a very grim time.

I shall always remember taking a phone call the following May 2010, from the Chief Constable of Sussex Police, with whom I had had some very difficult conversations over this case. He called to let me know that they were closing the case with no charges brought. Senior members of Sussex Police were among our guests when we reopened the hospital in July 2010 after a complete refurbishment and an intensive staff training and development programme. It was a low key but extremely rewarding day.

As I said at the beginning, suicide casts a long shadow. Because of the high-profile nature of these cases, it was several years before the inquests were held. This must have been desperately painful for the relatives. It was also hard the staff, who needed to learn from what had happened but also put it behind them so they could rebuild their confidence and get on with the vital work of caring for vulnerable people.

I sincerely wish that the media, who no doubt think they are serving the public interest in reporting prolifically on suicides of people who use mental health services, would think carefully when they publish such stories. Samaritans have produced excellent media guidelines[24] following extensive consultation and engagement with the media and the public. They include avoiding negative or stigmatising language, showing sensitivity and respect, and excluding details that might encourage copycat behaviours. I have no greater wish than that the media would use this guidance. The damage they can do by ignoring it is immeasurable.

And I wish the media would think about staff who make the very difficult choice to work in mental health services. The majority of people would not have the courage, compassion or patience to do it. It would help very much if the media would show respect for the distress that staff feel when they lose a patient to suicide – this is a person with whom they have often worked very hard, sometimes over many years, to keep safe.

As I complete the book, there is considerable media interest in increased sickness rates for stress, anxiety and depression among mental health staff. I have been invited onto BBC Radio 5 Live and various local BBC stations to talk about why this might be. While lack of resources, increased demand and scrutiny from inspectors and others may be factors, so too is how the media treats mental health services. We seldom see stories of staff doing wonderful work, as we do of physical health services. But when something goes wrong, the media goes to town. Imagine how it must feel to be pilloried for a tragedy that you desperately wish had not

---

[24] www.samaritans.org/media-centre/media-guidelines-reporting-suicide

happened. The media may think they are shining a light, but sometimes it is right into the eyes of people who are trying their best.

Towards Zero Suicide

Zero-anything policies are anathema to me. They seem aggressively negative and even set up to fail. But I have listened to people who think such a policy approach is helpful, and I was pleased to chair a conference in September 2017 called Towards Zero Suicide.These are the learning points that I took away:

- *Some of us are more vulnerable than others to thoughts of suicide. But with enough stress and pressure, almost anyone will think about it.*
- *Whether you have, as Sarah Hughes of the Centre for Mental Health described, made your peace with the term Zero Suicide, we can all embrace the hope behind the message. Because as Keith Waters of Derbyshire Health Care and the National Suicide Prevention Alliance reminded us, suicide is not inevitable.*
- *The long history of suicide in our society helps us to understand the shame still associated with it. And we still need to tackle that shame, because ultimately it can kill.*
- *There are no simple solutions to suicide prevention. It has to be locally relevant, dynamic and evolving. And it must involve everyone, from individuals to organisations, public and private. Those who traditionally resist engagement with suicide prevention strategies, such as coroners and the media, must be persuaded that they too have a part to play.*
- *While there are links to mental illness, most deaths by suicide are of people not in touch with mental health*

Towards Zero Suicide (cont.)
services. And yet suicide prevention is often seen as the sole responsibility of those working in mental health.

- *As Pippa Smith of British Transport Police said with great kindness and eloquence, a death by suicide is like no other. It touches not just those directly affected. And it can cause lasting damage.*
- *Removing the means to carry out a suicide can save lives. But at the same time, if applied without sensitivity, it can also remove a person's dignity, which may be the only thing they have left.*
- *Mental health first aid is as effective as physical first aid. So why is it not mandatory in workplaces, universities, schools, hospitals, public spaces and across society, including in mental health services, where staff sometimes lack the basic knowledge and skills to be effective in helping a suicidal person?*
- *Too much emphasis is placed on risk assessment. As Alys Cole-King so brilliantly put it, you cannot predict risk accurately. It differs from person to person and changes moment by moment. Instead, clinicians need the latest evidence so they can assess the person rather than the risk, and provide treatment and care accordingly.*
- *I loved Alys' idea that when someone is suicidal, emergency services would ring ahead, as they do for major physical trauma cases. But instead of asking for the resuscitation room to be made ready, they would say 'Please get the compassion room ready'.*
- *NHS crisis services are being reduced to save money, causing damage to clients and staff. Why is this not a national outrage?*
- *Third sector organisations such as Suicide Crisis, run by Jo Hibbens who spoke eloquently about the people they*

> *support and the lives they save, can be wonderful. But they need the safety net and professional support of statutory services. They are not a cheap alternative.*
>
> - *Suicide prevention apps, as we heard from Iain Murray, Choose Life Co-ordinator in Aberdeenshire, can really help to save lives. I loved how he has marshalled wide community support for this work.*
> - *Mental health staff are experiencing increased stress at work, according to investigative work done by Radio 5 Live recently. We cannot expect them to give compassionate care if they are not treated with compassion themselves. It seems so obvious, and yet...*

Samaritans

I first read about Samaritans in Reader's Digest when I was 11. I remember learning how they were founded by the Reverend Chad Varah and how they grew from a few volunteers at his East End church to become a national 24/7 service. I went on to read Monica Dickens' novel *The Listeners* and her collection of works by other authors relevant to the work of the Samaritans, co-edited with Rosemary Sutcliffe, *Is there Anyone There?* And I called them a few times myself from a red telephone box like the one on the front cover.

When I was 23, I applied to become a Samaritan. By then I was qualified as a nurse and training as a health visitor. During the Samaritan recruitment process, I was economical with the truth about my own experiences. I had brushed it all under my own psychological carpet, and at the time was not admitting even to myself that I had experienced either anxiety or depression.

I loved doing Samaritan shifts at the centre in Denne Road, Horsham, where the Horsham and Crawley branch are still based today. The calls could be distressing, but the other Samaritans were extremely supportive. There were a few who were young like me, but most were older, and many were retired. They were all, without exception, calm, kind, non-judgemental and skilled at helping people find hope and meaning in their lives.

In those days, we were discouraged from telling anyone other than our closest family that we were Samaritans; it was felt that to become known might discourage people one knew from calling. I accepted this at the time, and so it has only been recently when the rules changed and anonymity was superseded by confidentiality that I have felt it was OK to talk about my time volunteering as a Sam, as we used to be called.

I didn't leave Samaritans well, though. I was going through a bad patch and just didn't have what it took to face the demands of others on top of my day job as a health visitor. When I moved to Brighton, I left without giving a proper explanation. I have felt guilty about the manner of my leaving for many years.

And so, to celebrate my 60th birthday, in 2015 I decided to do something about it, and along with 25,000 others, completed Ride London, a 100-mile bike ride, in aid of Samaritans. I raised £5,000 and helped increase their profile via a couple of BBC news pieces that added somewhat to the pressures of the day. I did the same ride again for Samaritans in 2016, and the shorter 46-mile version in 2017, this time for my local branch.

And now I'm doing something else. During those gruelling eight hours in 2015, I realised that I was finally ready again to make my own regular, individual contribution to helping keep other people safe. In 2016, I reapplied and was accepted to retrain as a Samaritan. It was an amazing experience and I have been lucky enough to join a branch where I have made the most amazing friends. Volunteering can be tough but it is also very, very rewarding.

Mindfulness and Samaritans

Listening really carefully without judgement to someone in distress seems to me to be the very essence of mindfulness. I'm learning this while I develop as a Samaritan. Samaritans don't just learn how to do this once. We spend our first year in training. And then, however experienced we are, we listen very carefully to one another, in order continually to improve. Because we don't just care about our callers, we care about our fellow Samaritans.

A Samaritan shift can be the ultimate mindful practice. The room is peaceful and quiet. You listen, moment by moment, to your caller. You are listening in order to understand. You respond only when the caller seems ready, and use their words to reflect what you have heard. You give them space and time. You do not make suggestions and you do not judge. Your whole purpose is to be there with them while they explore their feelings and make their own decisions, if indeed they feel that any need to be made. The time simply disappears. At the end of your shift you debrief to another experienced Samaritan, not really about the calls, but how you handled them, what you might do differently another time and how you are feeling. You are reminded of the valuable service you have given. And you go away feeling calmer and lighter because of the mental discipline and compassion you have been practising. That is my sort of mindfulness.

Mindfulness and Samaritans (cont.)

Here are some wonderful listening tips, developed by Samaritans, that anyone can use:

1.Show you care

Focus on the other person, make eye contact, put away your phone.

2.Have patience

It may take time and several attempts before a person is ready to open up.

3. Use open questions

Use open questions that need more than a yes/no answer, and follow up with questions like 'Tell me more'.

4.Say it back

Check you've understood, but don't interrupt or offer a solution.

5.Have courage

Don't be put off by a negative response and, most importantly, don't feel you have to fill a silence.

You can learn more on the Samaritans website www.samaritans.org/media-centre/our-campaigns/talk-us/shush-listening-tips

In 2016, Samaritan volunteers had 5.5 million contacts by phone, email, text and face-to-face with callers. Demand for the service increases and we are make ourselves increasingly available. If you are feeling desperate, as I once was, please do call 116 123 or email Jo@Samaritans.co.uk. I have never met a Samaritan yet who doesn't exude quiet non-judgemental kindness. And don't worry, you almost certainly won't speak to me. Samaritans have a national telephone system and calls are directed to any branch where a volunteer is available. Callers speak to a Samaritan, rather than an individual. That is the beauty of the service, and how Samaritans can keep their promise to be available 24 hours a day, 7 days a week, 365 days a year, to listen and help people work out what to do for themselves.

Thank you and sorry

In closing this chapter, I would like to thank some people. To Professor Louis Appleby CBE and Dr Alys Cole-King, thank you for your ongoing work not only to reduce suicide but also to bring it from the shadows. You are wise, good people. You shine a light for others to follow.

To all my friends at Grassroots and Samaritans, thank you for teaching me that suicide can be prevented, and for supporting me to play my own very small part in helping people who are feeling desperate.

To all the people who lost someone while in the care of the trust I used to run, and to all the staff affected by suicide who felt in any way unsupported while investigations were underway or in the aftermath, I apologise unreservedly. I wish I could have made things better for you. I wish I could have done whatever was needed to help prevent the tragedy, and I wish I could have supported you better after it happened. But I also thank you, because I have learned a great deal by hearing about your experiences. And I hope I have become a kinder and more compassionate person because of them.

Chapter 12

My old unwelcome friend

I met my first psychiatrist when I was 15. And I've had various episodes of mental illness since then. Like a lot of people, I have not always described them as such, even to myself, at the time they were happening.

In writing this chapter, I have tried to explore why, despite my job running a mental health trust, it wasn't until I was 58 and approaching retirement from that role that I finally felt able to share a little of my experiences. And in particular, to be honest about what it was like to be a chief executive who didn't always feel OK, but felt that she had to pretend that she was.

I finally came out via an article in *Health Service Journal* entitled **A very personal 'Personal Best'** (2 October 2013). The article preceded an apparently sudden, significant depressive breakdown just a few weeks later. Was this coincidental? Very probably not. And did I get better after this episode as quickly as I led others to believe? Almost certainly not either.

Writing this book has been a significant part of my recovery. But like any recovery, it has not been easy. Nor has it been linear. I have mentioned elsewhere Rosebeth Moss Kanter's analysis of the 'difficult middles' of any project. I have been going through my own difficult middle. Getting all this stuff down on paper has presented a series of horrible hurdles. I have written and thrown out more pages than I have submitted for publication. I have had days when I felt that I couldn't go on. And I have caused myself pain as I poked and prodded in retrospect at my feelings about my life as a leader in the NHS.

But writing about my experiences has also been a source of solace and healing. I have reached certain conclusions and hopefully laid to rest some feelings about myself that were damaging and unhelpful. If you like writing, I do recommend it. It isn't easy but it gets things into the open, and sunlight is the best disinfectant. If you don't, then I imagine it would be the worst thing possible to try to write a memoir.

There are different sorts of writers. One difference I have heard others describe is whether they think everything through carefully first and then write it out later, or whether they allow the writing to dictate what they want to say via a process of trial and error. For me, with an extrovert preference in my personality, I work things out best by verbalising them. It doesn't have to be with another person, although that is of course rewarding; I have used writing to explore my thoughts throughout my life. This book has been the same - I didn't know I thought some of the things I have written about until I found myself putting them down.

Existentialism speaks of life being a series of possible branching paths one might take. The other branches exist in a different plane, and it is the human being him/herself who, through acts of will, decides which path to follow. I'm not sure life is as determined as this makes it sound. But nor is it totally random, as some believe. I am aware, as you will be for yourself, of decisions made, or in some cases decisions avoided, which have had a permanent impact on me and on others. With some of these decisions, one is aware of their momentous nature at the time. Others only become clear with the benefit of that marvellous but very rare instrument, the retrospectoscope.

Another major world philosophy, Buddhism, describes how there is no action, or inaction, that is without consequence. Although this can be a hard truth to bear, I find it helpful when making a decision about doing something difficult. Avoiding a decision is, in effect, also a decision.

It is only with hindsight that I realise one such seminal moment when I made a decision not to act. It was 2001, the year I was appointed chief executive at West Sussex Health and Social Care, the trust I was helping to set up. As Project Director, I had time to visit community groups to talk about the new trust and hear about the changes they hoped it might bring. One Saturday, I went to a meeting of a women's group in Crawley. We had a really interesting conversation about the hopes for the future held by these women, all of whom had either used or supported someone who had used local mental health services. And then we shared some lunch. Over sandwiches and samosas, one of the women said something to me along these lines: you seem really sympathetic and understanding; it is almost as though you have had your own experiences of mental illness. It wasn't really a question. She was far too sensitive to back me into a corner and ask me outright. We shared a knowing look. But the moment passed and somehow I had chosen to say nothing.

Until a few years ago, I would have described my lack of response as appropriate. Because this meeting wasn't about me, it was about them.

But with the benefit of hindsight, I am less sure. In 2016, I had the privilege to read the dissertation of my dear friend Odi Oquosa, which he wrote to complete his master's degree in social work. When I first met Odi in 2005, I would probably have described him as acutely psychotic. That he has qualified at master's level as a social worker is testament to his creativity, hard work, love of humanity and most of all, his courage. As Odi says in the introduction to his dissertation, a key turning point came when he was extremely ill. At that time, Odi lacked trust in any of the professionals who were supposedly caring for him. But then his own social worker took a personal and professional risk, and came out to him as gay, a major decision for the person concerned. This unusual but honest sharing had an impact because it enabled their relationship to move to a more equal footing. And it was this that made it possible for Odi to trust his social worker enough at last to accept help, and thus start his own remarkable recovery. Odi didn't just achieve his master's degree, he was also awarded top student of his social work year at the University of Sussex. He went on to be awarded national Social Work Student of the Year by *Community Care* magazine. And most importantly, he is now supporting adults and older people to live the fullest of lives.

So now I tend to see my silence back in 2001 as a lost opportunity. Who knows how I, or indeed the staff and services I led, would have fared had I decided to talk about my own experiences honestly from that time. A number of wise, kind people have told me that I have nothing to be ashamed of for not doing so. And I have come to accept that, for whatever reason, I wasn't ready then.

But I would nonetheless urge you, given that you are reading this, to give your own situation careful attention, and to try to bring the whole of yourself to work if you possibly can.

In the end, it will be much easier that way.

The costs of not being all of you: imposter syndrome

Imposter syndrome affects almost every leader at some point, apart perhaps from the ones who are sociopaths. And they don't read books like this anyway.

It was first described by psychologists in the 1970s. This is a nice definition, from Caltech Counselling Center:

'Impostor syndrome can be defined as a collection of feelings of inadequacy that persist even in the face of information that indicates that the opposite is true. It is experienced internally as chronic self-doubt, and feelings of intellectual fraudulence'.[25]

While it should stroke my ego to learn that imposter syndrome most seriously affects people who are hard-working high achievers, knowing this is not altogether helpful. The whole point of Imposter Syndrome is that you feel as though you are pretending all the time.

---

[25] http://wwwcaltech.edu

In other words, do I even have it? Or am I an imposter at being an imposter?

My imposter syndrome manifests itself in many unhelpful ways. One is that I dream vividly. The contents of other people's dreams are invariably tedious, but for the purpose of this exercise, I need to share. The night before something important is happening, or even when I am just anticipating something seemingly ordinary, I will dream about an unrelated occasion where I make a complete idiot of myself. In my dream, I turn up to a public venue with key items of clothing missing, even completely naked. And I have not done this by accident, I have made a conscious decision because I think I can get away with it and that no-one will notice. Or I appear in the first night of a play knowing none of my lines, or I am sitting an exam having not attended any of the lectures. Or I ask a foolish question in front of extremely well-read people which demonstrates that I am a charlatan and an idiot. Or I make a huge fuss about something trivial, escalating to shouting and other examples of bad behaviour, which is met with calm professionalism or polite indifference. It doesn't take a psychologist to work out that I have deep fears of being found out for being poorly prepared, lazy, ignorant, bombastic and ineffective.

And that is just the list I am prepared to share...

Writing the book has undoubtedly triggered some of these anxiety, work-related imposter syndrome dreams. Below is something I wrote midway through when I was in the US visiting family and feeling seriously fed up about the effect the book was having on my well-being and ability to concentrate on anything else.

Miami nice?

A deserted swimming pool on a cloudy Miami day. Cranes on the horizon. Wind tangling the palms. Water cools my skin. My mind swirling.

I'm not thinking as sharply as I would like at the moment. Although I can write; short pieces come easily. And stories queue impatiently, waiting for me to pay attention to them instead of the thing I am meant to be working on. It, the Opus, lies menacingly in my computer. In my mind it is self-indulgent, tedious, uninspiring.

A realisation: it has become my albatross. It feels stale and I don't like it. Digging around to create the chapters seems increasingly painful and pointless. Who will want to read such self-indulgent shit anyway?

At the same time, am I such a lazy shirker that the book I promised to write will never be finished? I fear this to be so.

Despite this, facing up to the fact that I have a choice over whether I abandon it feels freeing. I know, intellectually at least, that giving in to this feeling is not necessarily the act of laziness I harshly judge it to be. It might instead be my salvation.

The wind in the trees is whispering; I listen, but I can't quite hear what it is saying. Yet. I need to listen more.

I have grown sick of my dreams. Every night after working on The Thing, and often even after days when I have avoided looking at It, I am back at work, in another impossibly embarrassing situation that shows me in my poorest light. Always, my successor is there, calm and full of wisdom, as I never was. People hang onto his words but pay no attention to mine. I am petulant, shrill, imperious, irascible. And each time, as the dream sequence reaches its embarrassing conclusion, I realise that I should have left ages ago but have hung on, long past my sell-by date.

In these dreams, people humour me. They let me chair meetings and open things, but when I try to make anything of substance happen, I am politely ignored. My office has been moved to a forgotten space at the end of a long corridor, a disused attic, an abandoned building site. I have no-one to look after my visitors, no computer, no coffee. I am Mrs Nobody.

My soundtrack for the past few months has been Sufjan Stevens on loss and death from his latest album Carrie and Lowell. I have not lost a mother as he has. But I have had other losses. His music is tender and exquisite. It troubles and soars. I was a mess after seeing him perform at the End of the Road Festival in Dorset. I saw him again a few days ago here in Miami. The same thing is happening. I thought delving into those feelings helped. But now I wonder.

I listen to the trees some more. And I recall waiting at the start line on that August morning only three months ago when I cycled 100 miles in a day for Samaritans. As each group rode out, the organisers played requests. Someone from the group before ours had chosen Let It Go from the film Frozen. A far cry from Sufjan. It was in my head all day as I pedalled doggedly on. And it's coming back to me again. Perhaps that's what I have to do now. Let it go.

After all, the cold never bothered me anyway.

PS Back in England, it isn't quite as cold as I was expecting. But as I skate with clumsy enthusiasm around a deserted Royal

Miami nice? (cont.)

Pavilion ice rink for the first time since it opened for the 2015/16 season, I make myself two promises. This is the winter I am going to learn to skate backwards. And I am also going to finish this bloody book.

PPS Two years later, I can only just skate backwards. But the book is done.

Imposter syndrome and depression

Here's an interesting thing. While I get invited to give talks about depression, having now become known as a campaigner who is also an expert by experience, I feel troubled. Because deep down, my Imposter Syndrome extends to that aspect of my life as well. When I allow the Imposter Syndrome to take over, I believe that what overwhelms me from time to time, that sense of pointlessness, weariness, loss of joy or indeed any feeling at all other than deep and utter loathing towards myself, is not depression. It is just my own weak character. It isn't an illness. It is a fatal flaw in my psyche which, were I a better, less lazy and selfish person, I would not experience.

At one level, I find this ironic, a Catch-22 of my own creation. Intellectually, I know that the improvement I gradually experience when I go back onto antidepressants simply would not happen if I were faking depression. Modern antidepressants are not happy pills. They only work if your own serotonin is in short supply. If you don't need them, all they will give you is their side-effects, such as bleariness on waking, plus the more specific ones that come with the different formulations. I am lucky; I experience relatively few side-effects. Florid dreaming is one, but this continues when I come off the medication so perhaps I have just become a dreamer. When

I am depressed, I have no dreams at all. Mind you, with disturbed or minimal sleep, dreams are unlikely.

One of the things I have learned through therapy is that depression is not my usual state. I am naturally a joyful, positive person with a deep love for other people and the world in which we live. But I am at the same time someone with a tendency to depression. I am overly self-critical, a much harsher judge of myself than I am of others. This leads me to question whether, with hindsight, I was ever really cut out to be a chief executive.

But then I think of the thousands of amazing times that I spent with people who inspired me, the joy I felt on the majority of days during those 13 years about the work that I was lucky enough to do, and the sense of achievement that arose from things I have written about elsewhere in this book.

And I realise that to think I should never have done it is also part of the Imposter Syndrome. Almost anyone can become a chief executive. You just have to want to do it enough and care enough about the things for which you are responsible to be able to accept the more horrible and distressing parts of the job.

From my diary

Finally, here are a couple of pieces I have written since retiring and which hopefully round off what I've been trying to get across in this chapter.

September 2015

WELCOME BACK

Hullo you.

So you're back, are you? Please forgive me if I haven't exactly laid out the red carpet. It's just that the last time you were here, you caused havoc. It took me a year to deal with the consequences. You wore me out. My family and friends were extremely glad to see the back of you. My own feelings, as you well know, were more mixed. Because I recognised that you had, quite literally, become part of me.

What I can tell you, as you so cleverly insinuate yourself back into my life, is that I'm better prepared for you this time. I've done a lot of soul-searching. And I've had professional help. I have slowed down my thinking and learned the painful lesson of sharing, with a few trusted people, that I'm not always OK, and in particular the devastating effect you can have on me if I don't take care.

I've also made some new friends, who know you too, or someone like you. At great personal cost, they have developed ways of living in harmony with their cruel demon. I am indebted to the generosity of these new friends. I am even grateful to you, because, were it not for your last, most shocking visit, I would never have met these extraordinary people.

Yet again, I have only recognised your arrival with hindsight. A disapproving little voice whispering in my ear at my 60th birthday party, at the very moment I told those closest to me that I had finally got my mojo back, saying: have you? Have you really??

This makes me question myself. Was I pretending, all those months after I thought you'd left? Faking it till I baked it, as the saying goes? I don't think so. Because faking is almost impossible with you around. My razzle-dazzle, such that it is, fades in your presence. My smile becomes less convincing when it is painted on. Plus, and this has been a very important lesson, pretending hurts me. It also does damage to others.

This month, you appear a few times, in the small hours, when I should be turning over from the first refreshing sleep of the night and falling quickly back into the next slumber. Instead, I become alert and watchful. At these times, you make me go over past failings, magnifying them out of all proportion. In the mornings, there you are again, a dank blanket, ready to spoil the day. Not every day, but enough of them to make me worried that soon, you might not be leaving.

Most wicked one, you mess with my head. You have ways of making me feel responsible for everything that has ever gone wrong with anything that I have been remotely involved in, and for not doing enough to solve the ills of the world. You force to me go over and over stuff that makes me feel bad or sad, and guilty for my luck at any of the good things that have come my way. You tell me I am undeserving, selfish, lazy, intellectually weak, self-indulgent, tedious and evil.

And I believe you, to some extent, but not quite so much as before. Because I have learned about your psychological tricks. In a straight fight, I know you will always win. I need to listen to you, because occasionally you are right. After all, you are merely an extension of my conscience, aren't you? I just mustn't try too hard to placate you, or listen so much that I stop hearing other voices who speak more kindly to me.

As I've grown older, I've tried to take myself less seriously. To be less certain and to listen with greater care. And I've learned that to be kind to others, which after all is the whole point of having been put on this earth and being human, I must first be kind to myself. So I'm trying more of that now, mainly in my internal world, but also by sharing how I am feeling with those close to me and some of my newfound friends.

I'm not going to try to banish you from my life. I can't; you are a part of me. But please don't get big ideas. You are only a part. Not the whole of me. Despite your mean little voice telling me I don't deserve professional care, I have again sought it. It is already helping.

In the end it's up to me, and only me, whether I allow you to become my defining feature. I am determined that you won't be. To achieve that, I must also never again pretend that you don't exist at all. That is why I have written a version of this as a blog, for all to see.

I will face you, and not allow you to win by making me feel ashamed of your occasional visitations.Welcome back, my friend. Today the sun is shining, and you are quiet. But I know you are still there, waiting for me in my weaker moments. And I'm ready for you.

I hope.

With love from Lisa

A few days later I wrote this:

It is a daily challenge at the moment just to get by. Writing the letter and putting it on my blogsite was a release. Outing how I'm feeling means that as well as seeing my GP and therapist, I've forced myself to talk honestly with my family and a couple of trusted friends about not being on top of the world. I've reassured them that it isn't anything like as bad as what happened two years ago. But that I do need their help to keep my little demon under control. My husband decides we will do some regular hard walking and cycling in the autumn sunshine. My personal trainer is also firm on the importance of strenuous exercise, daily if possible. The children are lovely. I go swimming in the ladies' pond on Hampstead Heath with a friend who is kind enough to brave the icy water with me. Another takes me out for lunch and to augment my autumn wardrobe. I start an improver's knitting course. All this helps.

And as I turn back to my computer to get on with the book, I notice that Sussex Partnership have been entertaining the Shadow Secretary of State for Health and the new Mental Health Minister. There are some great photos. The sight of some of my wonderful ex-colleagues smiling into the camera hits me in the solar plexus. I miss them all so much, and love what they do. Being chief executive there was the best job in the world for me, most of the time.

But for the sake of the patients and the staff, and for my own sake, I am reminded that it was time for me to go. And that needing to leave so I could get on with my new life was, and remains, nothing to be ashamed of.

Letter to you, if you are experiencing depression

*This is a letter I submitted to the wonderful Recovery Letters [26].
During my depression in 2013/14, I couldn't read anything at all
for weeks. For a voracious reader like me, that in itself is a sign
of something being wrong. But I remembered having read about
the Recovery Letters on Twitter, and when I could, I made
myself read some of them. I then found myself doing so again,
many times. These letters, plus a book, The Curse of the Strong,
by Dr Tim Cantopher offered tiny rays of hope as gradually, I
began to realise that they were saying something directly to me
about how I would get better. I wrote the letter hoping it might
help someone else. Someone perhaps like you?*

Dear You

*Thank you so much for opening this letter. You probably won't
be reading much (if anything) at the moment. So I need to grab
your attention.*

*I want to tell you something. I have been where you are, or my
own version of it. Depression (or whatever you prefer to call
how you are feeling at the moment) is different for each of us.
And there are different sorts. But that really doesn't matter.
What makes you and me similar is the utter awfulness of our
experience. The weariness, even exhaustion, and yet inability to
sleep. Lying awake for hour after endless hour, either alone or
next to a partner who you can't tell about the darkness of your
thoughts. How pointless everything seems, especially in the
mornings. How things you used to look forward to seem trivial
and too much effort. How worried you are about things you
used not to worry about, and even more worried over things*

---

26 http://therecoveryletters.com/

that were worrying you already. And how loathsome and undeserving you feel, in every possible way.

Let me tell you a secret. When I was last ill, not all that long ago, I wanted to be dead. I even felt jealous of people with terminal illnesses like cancer because they had a reason for staying in bed and dying and people wouldn't think badly of them for it. And yet at the same time, I didn't really believe I was ill. I went along with my psychiatrist and GP because I thought I must, and I didn't have the energy to argue with them. But inside, I was convinced I was a lazy, work-shy, cowardly, incompetent, self-obsessed waste of space.

Now let's talk about you. You are a wonderful person, with many fabulous and interesting things that make you who you are. It is just that you have lost sight of these for a little while. From my experience of the Big-D (and I've had it a number of times, each different in its own vile way), the special things that make you who you are will come back. It is just that the strength, patience and hope you need to wait for them to come back is exactly what depression takes away from you. So right now everything may feel impossible. I truly know that feeling.Depression is an illness. It can actually be seen in the brain. It may get better on its own. But depending on how severe it is, that can take ages. However bad things seem right now, if you don't seek help they could get worse. You may have already found that it helps to talk to a friend, or call a helpline. If not, however hard it feels, please think hard about giving this a try.

Your GP can help you very much. He/she will help you decide if you need medication and/or a talking therapy, or a referral to more specialist services. If you are prescribed them, the new antidepressant medications work with your body to help you heal. Yes, they have side-effects. But so do antibiotics and you would probably take those if you had a serious infection.

People and websites who tell you that taking antidepressants is a sign of weakness honestly don't know what they are talking about. Please don't take advice from anyone who isn't a qualified doctor. If you are prescribed medication, I hope you will consider taking it as it tells you, including avoiding the things it says you should avoid while you are on it. And if you are referred for a talking therapy, or a group, please give yourself a chance, however anxious you are, and give serious consideration to going along.

I could write pages and pages about how you WILL get better. But your concentration is probably not great right now. Plus there are other lovely letters here that I hope you will also read. I just want to end with this. You will have good days and bad days. Slowly, you will notice that there are more good ones than bad ones. You will rejoice again in small things, like washing your face, a walk round the block, or the smile of a stranger. You will find things to do that give you a sense of achievement. I did jigsaw puzzles and very bad knitting. You can choose your own. Just make the tasks small and achievable. And relish what you have achieved.Most of all, learn how to talk about how you are feeling. Bottling things up is rarely a good idea. And be kind to yourself. From my experience, this is the hardest thing of all. Learning to be kind to ourselves can be a lifelong project. But if you aren't kind to yourself, it will be much harder to be kind to other people. So for that reason, it is really worth it.

Thank you and well done for reading this. It was a huge step. I wish you good luck on the rest of your journey. And please know this: you are not alone.

With my loving kindness for your gradual recovery

Lisa

Chapter 13

Leaving well?

Introduction: A bit of basic psychology

There is plenty written about the importance of leaving well. The psychological term for this is separation.

We begin to practise separation when we are very young children. We have to learn that when our mother/other main caregiver leaves us for the first time for a few moments, an hour or even a day, that she hasn't disappeared forever. It can be a hard lesson. We suffer separation anxiety. Sometimes we use transitional love objects, such as a teddy or a blanket, to help us get through this painful time.

For most children, the anxiety of separation substantially subsides when the child learns about the concept known as object permanence, which is that when the mother leaves, she hasn't disappeared forever and really will come back. But this doesn't happen in all cases, and is why the mental health prognosis for children who lose their mother before the age of 12, through abandonment, death, illness or by being removed from their care for legal reasons, can be problematic unless extra care and attention is paid to their psychological wellbeing. And it is why children's mental health services prioritise children who have lost their mother or other main carer.

Despite all the lessons learned as children, many adults will suffer from a form of separation anxiety from time to time, and for some it will be a major problem. They may experience leaving people or situations as painful and difficult. This can be manifested in relationships that end badly, with unnecessary pain or acrimony, or that don't end when they naturally should. Some people find it impossible to be on their own, and are over-reliant on others in work and/or social settings. Separation anxiety in adults can include excessive anxiety about change, including change of job or role. For such people, retirement can loom forebodingly.

It wasn't until my retirement approached that I realised I was experiencing more anxiety than I had anticipated. Knowing this didn't make the process less painful. But I hope that in telling it as truthfully as I can, again with the benefit of hindsight, I might help someone else. Someone like you, perhaps?

What does leaving well actually mean?

Leaving well is not as straightforward as it sounds. I read this nice piece by Frederick Schmidt in the *Huffington Post*[27] about retirement that focussed on psychological and spiritual wellbeing. It listed the key components for leaving well as these:

- If at all possible, anticipate leaving
- Identify the tasks that need to be completed
- Make the hard decisions that remain
- Let go
- Accept the freedom that comes with endings
- Embrace the future

Makes it sound really simple, doesn't it?

But the reality is that, for many public sector leaders, leaving is not an active choice. More often than not it happens to them, either because of a reorganisation or something that has gone wrong over which they must take ultimate responsibility. If you are facing such circumstances, there are only two tips that I can give you.

1. Act with dignity
2. Do whatever you can to give yourself control, if not over the whole of your work life, then of some aspect of it.

---

[27] www.huffingtonpost.com/frederick-w-schmidt/on-retiring-and-changing-jobs-leaving-well-as-a_b_7442014.html

Although I essentially orchestrated the reorganisation that created Sussex Partnership in 2006, and I was by then chief executive of two of the three predecessor trusts, I felt it was necessary to everyone concerned to put myself at risk so that I had to apply for the new job. It felt fairer and more above-board than being slotted in, never again getting that wonderful feeling of securing the job in my own right that I had experienced back in 2001.

BUT... it was one of the most public and potentially humiliating processes I have ever known. I was being judged by staff and peers. The prospect of failure was too embarrassing to contemplate.

I decided I was going to be dignified and get myself into good shape physically and mentally. So, for the two months leading up to the interviews, on 20 January 2006 , I went on an ultra-healthy diet, exercised every day, and prepared myself mentally as best I could. And of course, I bought a new outfit.

Over the two days of interviews, I recall the feeling of all eyes being on me. But I held my head up. And I'd like to think that had the outcome been different and my application been rejected, I would at least have felt that I gave it my best shot. I'd like to think....

The first time I decided to leave

When I think back to my first attempt at retiring from Sussex Partnership in 2010, I shudder. I made a very public mistake. And I got some ribbing for it. This is what happened.

All years bring their challenges for CEOs. But with hindsight, the year preceding my self-made debacle, 2009, sent more than usual in my direction.

It was the year after we became a foundation and teaching trust. The euphoria from that had gradually slipped away. Commissioners were looking for big savings (again). And we had a couple of changes in the executive team which were unsettling, especially for me.

But it was the two incidents that I mention in the final section of Chapter 10 that most troubled me at work that year. Looking back, I was experiencing trauma.

And this was because, alongside the pressures at work, I had some issues of my own at home. Our daughter, who had experienced atypical migraines for a number of years, was diagnosed with a serious abnormality in the blood circulation to her brain, requiring urgent neuro-surgery. I have never felt more frightened in my life than I was after going to see the neurologist with her or while waiting for her to come from theatre. She may have been 26, but she was still our baby.

So, looking back, the trigger for my decision over Christmas 2009 to retire early in the summer of 2010, when I was 55, arose from that lethal combination of unmanageable stress at work plus similar at home.

When I told my chairman about my plans, on my first day in the office at the beginning of January 2010, he was visibly taken aback. He asked me if I was sure. But I can be pretty persuasive. I insisted not only that I was, but also that I should tell the non-executive directors the same day, and the executive team the day after. We then made a low-key public announcement. People were clearly shocked. And I had some lovely messages.

But it was not long before the negative media started. I was apparently leaving because I couldn't face the consequences of the police investigation. It wasn't true. But I didn't want to talk about my daughter, and anyway if you had asked me at the time, I could not have articulated how I was feeling. So I just had to suck it up.

Roll forward a few months. Alice had her first procedure at the National Hospital for Neurology and Neurosurgery, Queens Square, London in February 2010.

I can recount every moment of that long day; it was almost unbearably poignant to be wandering up and down Great Ormond Street, the scene of some happy but also desperately sad times when I was a young woman myself, as we waited for news. The procedure wasn't nice, but it went OK. I'm glad we didn't know then that she would need another four such procedures that year, and that she wouldn't get the all-clear until her 28th birthday. Although none of them were as bad as that first time, at least not for me. She had a rare condition but she was young and otherwise fit and healthy, and she had the best people looking after her. All hail our amazing NHS, this is the stuff it does best of all.

The relief was immense. And suddenly the police investigation faded to what it was, just colleagues doing their jobs because some awful things had happened, while we continued to do ours. The work to refurbish the affected hospital got underway, and the staff settled down to their redeployed roles and began to appreciate having time out to develop together before the new service opened. And I found myself driving into work in the mornings with a song in my heart which would then suddenly stop as I realised how little time I had left in a job that I still loved.

And I realised that resigning had been a terrible mistake.

I fantasised for nearly a month about telling people that I had changed my mind. But it felt too late for that. Recruitment for my replacement was well underway, and I was taking calls from some wonderful candidates to give them the lowdown on a job that I secretly felt should still be mine.

I would also be standing down as chair of the Mental Health Network, although not before leading the process on behalf of the NHS Confederation trustees to appoint our new chair. And I remember sitting alongside my fellow trustees early in April 2010 and interviewing some extraordinarily well-connected candidates, included Sir Keith Pearson, who said that at the age of 62 he still had at least one big job left in him. Keith was so knowledgeable and inspiring that I remember kicking myself; I wanted to work with him very much indeed.

That same week, back at the trust, the chairman and I interviewed Dr Tim Ojo, who had been our acting medical director since the previous autumn, and was now applying for the permanent job. And I remember thinking that I had spent eight years working with medical directors who for various reasons felt torn between their clinical careers and medical leadership. But here was someone with the vision and integrity to balance both, who would bring something very special to the table because of his innate goodness, courage and vision. And I was going to be leaving in just a few short months and wouldn't have the pleasure of seeing him blossom and making the impact that I believed he had the potential for. I was in tears when I finally got home that night. What had I done?

The week of the chief executive interviews arrived. I felt desperately unhappy but used the skills I had honed over many years not to show it. And then on the afternoon before the first of two days of focus groups and psychometric tests, I was crossing the carpark on one of our main sites with our vice chair, the wise and lovely Mike Viggers, who went on to become chair at Western Sussex Hospitals NHS Foundation Trust. Mike asked me if I was having any second thoughts. And I looked at him, and found myself saying that I was. And he said really? And he asked would I be prepared to stay for a while longer. And I said that I would, and so he rang our chairman John Bacon. And the interviews were cancelled.

And that was how it came to pass that when John was asked by the local media how much he had spent on the recruitment process, he said it had cost £20,000 but it had been a good investment because he had been able to appoint the right chief executive. This is why John was such a great NHS leader; he is incisive and supportive and has a brilliant turn of phrase.

But although I was on cloud nine because of this miraculous eleventh hour reprieve, I felt very bad about it. Especially for the candidates who were stood down the night before the selection process began.

And so I promised my board and made a vow to myself that I would do better the next time I decided to retire.

Footnote:

Whatever you might have read on social media or in the comments sections of online publications, my reason for withdrawing my resignation wasn't anything to do with the police eventually dropping the investigation into the unexpected deaths without bringing any charges. When I made my decision to stay after all, I realised that, whatever happened, not only could I cope, but that it was actually my job to stay and face whatever ensued. And although it was potentially terrifying, I wanted the opportunity to defend what needed defending, and to apologise unreservedly to the people affected for things that shouldn't have happened.

It was over a month after I had rescinded my notice that I got a call, completely out of the blue, from Martin Richards, then chief constable of Sussex Police. He said that his colleagues had finished their enquiries and that there would be no charges brought. I will be forever grateful to Martin for his kindness in making that call, especially as I had been pretty unpleasant over the initial decision to investigate us. Martin is a good man. And I am impressed that he is now a non-executive director at Sussex Partnership. Like so many friends in the police, he sees mental health as a shared business.

To everything (and everyone) there is a season

I will now roll forward through the years.

If 2010 was my year of not leaving after all, 2011 was the year that the still relatively new coalition government launched its mental health strategy, No Health Without Mental Health. As chair of the Mental Health Network, I was invited to speak at the launch event alongside health minister Paul Burstow and others about my hopes for the future. I said that the stigma experienced by people affected by cancer in 1942 when my mother's father died of the disease would be deeply shocking to us now. Waiting times for cancer diagnosis and treatment are top priorities and Cancer Research and Macmillan Cancer Relief are two of our biggest health charities. I said wouldn't it be wonderful if we could get to the same place for mental illness diagnosis, treatment, care and support, and truly eradicate the stigma of mental illness. And I said that I didn't want to have to wait another 68 years. So we needed to do something different now. And everyone clapped and *seemed* to agree.

The new year, 2012, started well for me, with the news that Sussex Partnership had achieved fourth place in the prestigious Stonewall Workplace Equality Index, the highest ever position for an NHS organisation (see Chapter 8.) And in April, I got that letter from the Queen asking me if I would be prepared to accept the honour of becoming a Commander of the British Empire. It was lovely when it was announced in the Queen's Birthday Honours in June 2012, and I had the inauguration in January 2013 to look forward to. But in August 2012, we had the awful incident at our hospital in Crawley, and I felt deeply responsible for the dreadful thing that happened and for the collusion afterwards (See Chapter 10.) This made me think hard over Christmas and I decided it was getting close to me needing to think about doing something different.

The following year, 2013, also started well, when we beat our own position and came second in the Stonewall Index. I went to the Palace and wrote a blog that said I wasn't always CBE material. It got such positive reactions that I knew I needed to say a bit more, once I felt free to do so. I also appeared in the *Health Service Journal* list of inspiring women leaders. Plus, we won the *Health Service Journal* Research impact award (see Chapter 8).

Having made such a mess of it the previous time, I planned my second retirement announcement with military precision. Although

I was only required to give six months' notice, I wanted to give a year because I know how long it can take to recruit chief executives.

The announcement about my plan to retire in the summer of 2014 was made in September 2013. A few weeks later, I wrote that piece for the *Health Service Journal* about my experiences of anxiety and depression off and on since the age of 15. The responses were heart warming, if a little overwhelming. Nonetheless, if you had asked me how I was doing at the start of October 2013, I would have told you I had everything pretty well sussed.

But as I mention in the introduction to this book, this was when my metaphorical wheels started to come off. Looking back on how I was that month, I see now that I was as high as a kite, and not in a nice way. My team had seen me like this before, but not nearly as bad. Some of them thought it was an advance reaction to leaving, which in a way it was. What they didn't anticipate was the crash that came in that first week of November 2013. And despite the article and my apparent self-knowledge, no-one was more surprised than me.

You can read more about me and my relationship with depression in Chapter 11. For the purposes of this chapter, which is about leaving well, I will just say this. As I sat huddled on the sofa during the last two months of 2013, with the curtains closed because I was too ashamed to be seen, I thought I would never go back to work. I had totally blown it. And my greatest regret, which I shared with the members of my team who courageously came to see me and coped with the weeping mess that confronted them, was that I had let everyone down, and that nothing I had personally achieved had been anything other than useless. Where I previously thought I had been successful, I now realised that my success had been achieved not because of me but despite me, and was based entirely on the efforts of others.

But slowly, as 2013 ebbed away, and just as my GP and psychiatrist promised, the medication started to work. I began to sleep again. I felt tiny glimmers of pleasure at small things, such as the company of our cat William who had no formal training as a pet therapist but seemed to know exactly what was required of him. Gradually the really bad days became less frequent. I started creeping out of the house with my hood up and doing a lot of walking, initially after dark, and then tentatively, during daylight hours. And I began to think that maybe I could go back to work after all, and leave properly in the summer of 2014 as planned.

With a huge amount of help, that is what I did. I've written briefly about that first week in the introduction to this book. When I have to face anything difficult now, and as I know I will in the future, I have those memories to draw on. Having come out about my past experiences of depression only a month before I went off sick, it felt vital that all our staff knew why I was away from work. But even though people were lovely, going back made me feel like Exhibit A, totally depleted of the reserves I needed to cope with it[28].

Nothing will ever feel harder than walking into our headquarters on that first day and saying hello to people. And then later that week, standing up in front of our 200 most senior clinicians and managers and telling them I was back, and on the road to recovery, but to please bear with me.

To do this, I used cognitive behavioural therapy (CBT) techniques. These teach you to face up to the hard things, notice them, not over-think them, get on with dealing with them, and then reflect in an unemotional way and, if necessary, and it invariably is, to carry out the same exercise over and over again. You become your own walking experiment.

---

[28] Top tip: this is how most people feel when going back to work after a bout of depression. The way that colleagues and managers respond can make all the difference between it being hard but achievable, or an unnecessarily brutalising, even fatal, ordeal.

And that is really how I approached my final eight months. Once I had acclimatised to working full-time again, I decided to take control of my diary, go to fewer meetings, and spend more time with staff and the people we served. And to go home at a reasonable time. I set aside time for writing, and I did a great deal of listening. Because I wanted to make sure my successor had some insights that only I could give.

And I planned my leaving speech, which comprised tea and an awards ceremony for me to thank people, with hand-drawn badges based on our values, courtesy of my talented colleague Dr Mandy Assin. And I shared a list of things I was going to do next, one of which was to write this book.

I can truthfully say, as I come to the end of these outpourings, that I love my new life. I write - not only this book, but also my blog, articles, plus my "still-to-be finished-but-very-much-a-work-in-progress" novel. I coach people who somehow find their way to my door, help to run the Mary Seacole Trust, and speak from a personal perspective at conferences and other events on leadership and mental health, particularly raising awareness and reducing stigma.

And I have more time now to make jam, volunteer with Samaritans, ride my bike, grow things in the garden, help my mum and spend time with other family and friends, all of which are good for my own mental health.

So in the end I can truthfully say that I did the last three things on the list: letting go; accepting the freedom that comes with endings; and embracing the future.

I'm not sure that you could describe the overall experience as 'leaving well'. But in the circumstances, I did the best that I could.

The story of the three brown envelopes*

Many of you will already know this story, or a version of it. No-one seems to know where it originated, but it has appeared in many forms. It is a pretty dystopian view of organisational change, but I never tire of it. This is the way I like to tell it.

And by the way, not a single word of it is true.

A chief executive of a mental health trust is retiring after 13 years. She is handing over to her successor. She wishes him luck and tells him that she has left 3 brown envelopes in a drawer for him, numbered 1 – 3. She tells him that she has put them in there to help him. And she says that, when things get tough, as they are bound to do at some point in the future, she recommends that he opens the first envelope, as there will be something written inside that will be useful. And again, at a later point, if and when things get tough again, to open the second envelope, and that there will also be something inside this one that will also be useful. And the same with the third envelope. But to be sure to open them in the right order.

So, she leaves and goes off to write the book she has been banging on about. And the new chief executive breathes a sigh of relief that he has finally seen the back of her. He starts settling into the new job.

It goes really well to begin with. But after a while, things start to happen that worry him. Perhaps the CQC do an inspection which doesn't go as well as he had hoped. Or there is an incident with negative media coverage. Or some of the governors aren't happy with the quality of information they are getting.

So he goes to the drawer and opens the first envelope. And the piece of paper inside says this:

Blame your predecessor.

So he does, and it works for a while. People tell him that she was never any good, and that he was brought in to fix the mess she left behind. Things seem to settle down again.

But only for so long. After another year or thereabouts, the not-so-new chief executive finds he is struggling again. Maybe the money has got even tighter than it was when he started. And there are more patients than beds, staff and community services available. Or the commissioners say they need to disinvest in specialist mental health services and save millions of pounds by asking a third sector organisation to open a crisis café.

So he decides he may as well turn to the second envelope. And he goes to the drawer and opens it. The piece of paper inside says this:

Do a management restructure.

So he does. It gives him a focus, creates considerable disruption and distracts him and others from the things he was worrying about. It takes about a year to complete. Gradually, everything settles back down again.

But it is not long before he is worried again. Maybe the negative media won't go away. Or other bad things happen, such as a recruitment crisis, or some new governors are elected who are antagonistic to the strategy that he and the board have been developing. Or he has just grown tired and is experiencing a loss of enthusiasm, which can happen to any leader from time to time.

And so he goes to the drawer and gets out the third brown envelope and opens it. The piece of paper inside says this:

Get three brown envelopes.

To everything, and everyone, there is a season.

Chapter 14

Some closing thoughts

The original title for this book was Becoming a chief executive: What They Never Told Me (Or If They Did, I Wasn't Listening). For me, that title said it all. But people said it was too long.

Then I moved to the working title we used while I was writing the book, Tales of a Recovering Chief Executive, for which I have Professor Sir Simon Wessely, past president of the Royal College of Psychiatrists, to thank. It arose from a conversation we had in 2016. If you had told me in 2013 that this is what I might call my book, I would not have believed you.

During the time of writing, I undoubtedly have been a recovering chief executive. The book has been a form of self-directed therapy. If you have managed to read all the way through, you will have noticed that, as happens during recovery from anything of significance, the path was not always smooth. And I experienced a number of setbacks along the way.

Am I still a recovering CE? On some days, undoubtedly so. And on others, I relish what I am doing now so much that I can barely remember what my old life was like.

This is the nature of recovery. As is having the courage to go back to my original title, with a tiny tweak from Becoming to Being. Because I am not as flaky as I sometimes let myself believe, and I do sometimes have good ideas.

To future NHS leaders, with love

1. *You can learn all the improvement methodology you like. But If you forget that culture **always** trumps strategy, your efforts to improve services will be ineffective. I've been there and occasionally done it the right way. But more often the wrong way.*
2. *You can't help others to improve unless you are OK yourself. I have form when it comes to not remembering this.*
3. *Leadership in public services has never been harder with our 24/7 media, including social media, and the anti-public sector rhetoric that appears in most newspapers. We live in a post-fact world. People believe things that are not true, and don't believe things that are. I've had personal experience of this. And it is horrible.*
4. *Being an NHS leader is very lonely, never more so than when you are awake at 3 am worrying. People get in touch to congratulate you when something goes well. But when things go wrong, people you thought were friends seem to melt away.*
5. *There is never enough time to think when you are running NHS services because of competing demands, often from those who are meant to be there to help you make improvements. Despite this, you must create time to think or you will make bad decisions.*
6. *Filling senior vacancies in the NHS is getting harder. And we should worry about this. Because if we aren't careful, the only ones who apply to be in the firing line will be those who really don't care what others think about them. And that would be very bad for all of us.*
7. *We cannot separate leadership from mental health. In my opinion, people who experience mental illness from time to time can make exceptional leaders. It is only one of the things about them. In fact, they can develop skills*

through therapy that it would be hard to learn any other way – such as managing their own mood, listening really carefully, and not making assumptions about what others think.

8. *I have experienced depression off and on since the age of 15. A nurse said something damaging to me when I was 22 and vulnerable and which I absorbed deep into my psyche. For the next 36 years I stigmatised myself, despite being an active campaigner against the stigma of mental illness. It was only when I finally came out about my experiences that I was able to address my self-stigma. I have made many friends since then. But if only I had done it before, I could have been a far better, more authentic leader.*

9. *Mental illness messes with your head. It affects one in four of us. But four in four of us should care about it, not just on humanitarian and economic grounds, but because almost everyone can be affected. We are all on a spectrum of resilience, and if enough bad things happen to us, especially at a young age, most of us will experience post traumatic damage.*

10. *When I appeared suddenly to get ill with an acute onset of depression in 2013, it was a culmination of things, my own susceptibility, but also workload, loneliness, weariness as I approached retirement, not taking care of myself, listening too hard to my own negative voices, and putting a lot of energy into maintaining a positive front. It wasn't caused by internet trolls. But they didn't help.*

11. *So please don't do what I did. Get to know yourself. Talk to yourself honestly about how you are. Talk to your loved ones. Take care. Be the best version of you, but make sure that it is who you really are. And try always to see yourself as an improvement project – this makes it easier to accept criticism without it cutting you to*

> *To future NHS leaders, with love (cont.)*
>
> your core. I've only learned this in the last few years,
> and it has been a revelation!
> 12. I am extremely privileged. I have dear family and
>   friends. And I received great care. I was able to get
>   better and go back to a job that I loved, which was a
>   major part of my recovery. I know it isn't the same for
>   everyone. But it should be.

What are the attributes needed for the modern NHS chief executive?

As must happen to all writers, events occur at the time of writing that can seem highly relevant to the subject matter in hand. But one has to be careful. I have hesitated to include too many current examples to avoid dating this book. I try to use my blog for the more topical stuff. But I am minded to mention the interesting but, to me, deeply disturbing case of the dispute between the government and England's junior doctors, because it illustrates the overall point I want to make about being a chief executive or any type of leader in today's NHS.

It would be difficult to have missed the dispute over junior doctors' pay and conditions during the latter months of 2015 and throughout 2016. As I was writing the latter part of the book, it was top of the news. After protracted negotiations with both sides badmouthing the other in public, it was announced that a pay 'settlement' would be imposed, given that extended negotiations have failed to reach a conclusion satisfactory to all parties.

A brave group of young doctors used themselves as a test case and challenged the government's right to impose a settlement without negotiation via the courts. Several hundred junior doctors took it in turns to camp outside the headquarters of the Department of Health, attempting to doorstep The Right Honourable Jeremy Hunt MP, current secretary of state for health. He took to leaving from a side entrance.

The fallout from the Brexit vote in June 2016, and the subsequent change of prime minister left only Mr Hunt remaining in the same cabinet position. We shall never know if the rumours that he had not been the new PM's first choice for that role were true. And many of us wondered how long he might last in a role that he was widely reported to have been appointed to by the previous PM in order to neutralise the toxicity created by Andrew Landsley.

We thought it might depend on whether the sympathies of the public remained weighted towards the doctors. A deal was offered which some have accepted and some rejected. The chief negotiator from the British Medical Association resigned. And morale among junior doctors, already worryingly low, dipped further.

I know many junior doctors, the daughters and sons of friends and those I meet directly through my continued contact with the NHS. These young people, who hold other people's lives in their hands on a daily basis, are super-bright. Most of them are also sensible, compassionate, committed and driven. There will be the occasional charlatan, as in any group, but I can't think of any that I know. It is hard to understand how a secretary of state who was brought in to settle down the NHS after the mess created by the previous one could have allowed himself to get into dispute with this group of NHS staff, who enjoy so much public trust and sympathy.

I don't personally buy the conspiracy theories that the government's purpose for the dispute was privatisation by stealth; there would be better ways to achieve that than by annoying a popular and essential section of the workforce. Nor do I believe that anyone in public service could be as Machiavellian as some suggest, with the dispute a modern-day equivalent strategy similar to the one used by Margaret Thatcher to break the will of the miners.

It is far more likely to have been a cock-up. Someone probably advised the secretary of state that the existing contract was, as most senior NHS managers including those who are doctors knew, overly complicated and no longer fit for purpose. If indeed it ever was. This is of course not the fault of the junior doctors. And so Mr Hunt decided to cement his place as a moderniser and spearhead the introduction of a new one. But because he isn't a manager himself, he did so without understanding that the only way ever to introduce a new contract with any group of professional staff, whoever they may be, but especially doctors who have one of the most effective trade unions in the country to support them, is to improve on their current terms and conditions. There is nothing that upsets people more than attempts to introduce changes that worsen their position. And at the heart of it, it seems, is the fact that for everyone else in the NHS, Saturdays are not part of the core working week. Although there is little choice for the majority but to work on at least some Saturdays, doing so incurs additional payment.

The secretary of state also allowed himself to fall into a communications trap by talking about a seven-day NHS, when the group he was targeting were already working shifts across seven days. He chose the wrong target. To achieve a true seven-day service, he would need to persuade receptionists, secretaries, laboratory technicians, physiotherapists, plus those nurses and doctors from departments and specialties that don't work across seven days, to start working on a seven-day rota. It would mean employing at least 20 per cent more staff to cover these new shifts. And that would cost a great deal of money, which is the opposite of what the NHS has or is likely to have in the foreseeable future.

What I hear from my junior doctor friends is also the context of why they are so upset. And I think that this is forgotten at both sides' peril.

Doctors are human beings like everyone else. They deserve to be treated fairly and to work in conditions that allow them to have a life. But those who have planned and constructed the current system for allocating the work of junior doctors appear to treat them as though we were in a previous century and employment law did not exist. It is extremely difficult to get onto a training programme that takes account of personal circumstances. These young professionals are already in their late 20s. They have slogged away for ten years plus to get to where they are now. Only the most elite get the pick of training jobs in university teaching trusts. Everyone else is bundled around the country to placements that have to be filled, lasting only four months during the first two years, and, even towards the end, only a year. They are the workhorses of our NHS. They are highly intelligent adults. But they are treated like recalcitrant children. They are frequently expected to cover vacancies and other gaps in medical rotas caused by sickness or maternity leave as well as doing their own work, often at short notice. This plays havoc with personal relationships and family life. They are not a group for whom losing what little control they had over their working lives plus a substantial reduction in earnings (on salaries that are much less than the public imagine) would be likely to go down well.

With all this in mind, chief executives in trusts have a bottom line, which is to deliver safe services within the money available. And 20 of them, many of whom I know, were put in an invidious position over the dispute with the junior doctors. These 20 were representative advisers to NHS Employers, who act on behalf of all trusts in such negotiations. They were asked whether the offer that was made prior to the latest one was fair and reasonable. And on replying that, on balance, they felt that it was, they found their names being included in a letter from the chief negotiator to the secretary of state suggesting that they were in favour of an imposed settlement.

For the sake of the point I am making, it doesn't really matter whether this was cock-up or conspiracy either. Although I'm pretty certain it was a mistake, and the result of hurried drafting when people were tired and desperate to get something out. Mistakes are far more common than conspiracies. Humans make mistakes, and humans under pressure make them even more.

The letter caused a flurry on social media. And these good people had to decide whether to keep quiet, incurring the wrath of their own junior medical staff and indeed others who support the doctors, or to come out and say that they had not agreed to the imposition, potentially putting their own careers at risk. That the majority did the latter fills my heart with hope for the NHS.

And the point of telling you this story is this.

To be a leader in today's NHS, there are never going to be any right answers. You will frequently be faced with dilemmas of this nature. If you don't have the nous to know when to put your head above the parapet and when to stay quiet, the courage to do the right thing at the very time it seems most dangerous for you personally to do so, the confidence to trust people to do things themselves, the generosity to make sure they get the accolades when things go well and the guts to take the flak when they don't, and most of all the humility to admit when you have made a mistake, you don't have what it takes to run part of our precious, creaking, world-class-in-places-but-in-need-of-urgent-surgery-in-others NHS.

My worry is that there are not enough people with these attributes who want to do these jobs. And we really, really need them.

The *Daily Mail* test

Building on what I've just said about the balance of nous, courage and humility, I will return briefly to my *Daily Mail* test, which I mentioned earlier in the book.

My test can be applied to any challenge one faces in life. But as I hope I have already illustrated, chief executives in today's cash-strapped, highly politicised, performance-driven and multi-media exposed NHS where everyone has an opinion about everything, will come across such wicked questions more frequently than perhaps senior leaders in banks or IT companies.[29]

The test goes like this. You are faced with a seemingly impossible decision about doing x or y. In the case above, x is staying quiet and y is speaking out. Or it might be that x is forcing through a change that you are unsure of but that is being imposed upon you by a regulator, whereas y is arguing against that change with the regulator and risking your organisational reputation and possibly your own career. You have to make a choice. And as I have said before, it is useful here to remember one of the central tenets of Buddhism, which is that every action *or inaction* (my italics) carries a consequence. In other words, there is rarely a *do nothing* option.

The *Daily Mail* test is that you might appear on the front page of that newspaper, which is not known for its love of the NHS or even more so, its managers. The question you must ask yourself is, for which of these wicked choices would I rather be publicly pilloried in the *Daily Mail*?

---

[29] I'm not saying these jobs don't bring challenges. But making the wrong decision in such a job is less life-and-death or career limiting than running a trust. And salaries are usually many times higher. In 2016, the Head of Google Europe told the Public Accounts Committee that he couldn't remember how much his own remuneration package was. Either he really couldn't, in which case he is an idiot and has no right to be in charge of anything. Or, more likely, he was dissembling because he knew it to be an embarrassingly high sum, especially with Google under fire for paying very little corporation tax. Chief executives of trusts have their salaries published every year and get lambasted about the apparently obscene sums in newspapers like the Daily Mail. And they all know exactly how much they earn, which is a tiny fraction of the man from Google, but with many times greater responsibility.

If you don't know the answer, it doesn't make you a bad person. But it almost certainly means that being a chief executive in today's NHS is not for you.

Choosing mental health

As I said in Chapter 1, I'm not sure that I really chose mental health. I think it chose me. I can say with the benefit of hindsight, and obviously this is only my opinion, that it is the most difficult, frustrating, unfairly treated but also most rewarding part of the NHS. It is not for the fainthearted. Nor is it for those who struggle with complexity, lack of clarity or who do not relish having to fight for the sake of others who cannot fight for themselves.

And there is one specific difference which warrants inclusion, as I take my final look back. In no other part of health care is it the case that clinicians and managers have the power to give patients treatment against their expressed wishes, unless they lack capacity. There is nothing more serious that can be done legally to another person than to hold them against their will, when they have not committed any crime, in order to enforce treatment. Around 50 per cent of acute mental hospital admissions are made using the powers of the Mental Health Act.

The term 'compliance' has been used a great deal in the past within mental health services, referring to whether a patient is taking their medication, accepting their detention, co-operating with their care plan, among other things. It is also a term used frequently by regulators. And I don't like it. It implies passivity, hopelessness and lack of ambition, of accepting the status quo. For me, the things people who experience mental illness need most of all are hope and ambition, as do those who care for them, those who commission and those who run mental health services. No-one achieves recovery without hope.

I certainly didn't.

Being an NHS Chief Executive

My personal crisis about the state of mental health care

The NHS England sponsored Mental Health Taskforce report was published at long last in February 2016. The report pulled no punches about the state of services nor in identifying what needs to change. I take my hat off to Paul Farmer, CBE, chief executive of Mind, who led the work. It was undoubtedly a massive ask to get agreement from so many parties about what to include.

It is good that the report was so hard hitting. Occasionally we need a solid dose of the truth. But it is also deeply demoralising for those currently working in mental health services, knowing that whatever they do cannot meet the needs of everyone who needs help, and that much of their effort is either insufficient or futile.

For those using mental health services, who have for years been making the case that help is not as forthcoming nor as good as it should be, the report confirmed that they were right. But it is also frustrating, in that it says little that is new. And the financial promises made in response to it remain, at best, opaque.

From a personal perspective, I note my own combination of anger and frustration on reading and gradually digesting the report. Even now, there is a row between journalists I trust and government spokespeople about whether there really is any truly 'new' money, with contradictory statements flying about, on the back of definitive evidence that mental health trusts have seen real terms cuts in funding yet again in the last year, even though these were again strenuously denied by commissioners and government ministers at the time. It provides even more evidence of the stigma towards people who experience mental illness and to the services that struggle to help them. The wider row about NHS funding that heralded the start of 2018 only serves to press mental health further into the shadows. It encourages commissioners to ignore the requirement to reverse previous mental health cuts because nothing trumps waiting times targets (which don't apply to mental health services) or people waiting on trolleys in A and E, even though many of them will be affected by some form of mental illness, drug or alcohol problem.

Anger and frustration are often manifestations of guilt. And I realise that I feel guilty because in the end, despite my privileged position, relatively high profile and ability to speak with deep knowledge, I didn't make the difference I felt I should or could have made. And I wonder whether my apparently sudden-onset of depression in the year before I retired was to some extent a reaction to this sense of guilt about not having been able to be more effective in persuading politicians and commissioners that mental health services deserved a better deal than they got under my watch.

As I reach the end of this chapter, I cannot absolve myself of this guilt, but I do forgive myself, because I did try my best.

At least, that is what I do on a good day.

Is that all there is?

Before closing, I have tried to capture the essence of that strange feeling that comes to all of us who have had the privilege of a fulfilling career. And when you realise that the best of it seems suddenly to be in the past, but you hadn't noticed it passing.

I'm trying to describe how it feels to have reached your personal pinnacle, with the only way being down, and not even to have realised that it was a pinnacle at the time because you were so busy. To have become yesterday's woman or man. And to know that people are no longer as interested in what you have to say as they were when you were in your prime.

Most of us don't know we have achieved our pinnacle, except in retrospect.

There are some late starters, often women, who find peaks to ascend that were previously hidden from view. Dame Carol Black said on *Desert Island Discs* that she didn't feel she even got started on her career until she was 50. And at 77, she felt she had a great deal more to give. My friend and neighbour Jane Lythell had her first novel published aged 60, and has just published book number four. The wonderful Judith Kerr is still creating new characters to delight children of all ages at the age of 94. Oh, that I could emulate these admirable, inspiring women.

In Anne Karpf's book *How to Age*, part of the *School of Life* series, she puts forward the view that people are happier in their seventies than in their sixties because they have had time to get used to this apparent loss of status and incorporate a less achievement-focussed way of being into how they see themselves. But she also says that retirement can be very bad for us, and that most of us need to stay busy and feel useful. Holidays are wonderful because they are just that – breaks from the norm. To do nothing of any apparent value day after day, apart from pleasing oneself, is unlikely to be satisfying for people who previously shouldered significant responsibility

With hindsight, realising that my own peak had come and gone was in all probability a contributory factor in the episode of severe depression I experienced in 2013.

But that episode also served a purpose. After the initial weeks of ghastliness, I dragged myself out of bed and did a lot of walking. And as I pounded the winter pavements with my hood pulled up, wearing an old pair of glasses in the hope I wouldn't be recognised, I forced myself to start facing up to my future. Not just the immediate future that involved going back to work for another eight months, but what I was going to do – and be – afterwards.

And from the muddle in my mind, a reality gradually emerged. How lucky I was that I could perhaps forge a new career as a writer and mental health campaigner, with enough time to mentor and coach a few people, volunteer with charities and projects I cared about, and spend more time with friends and family.

I also realised what I didn't want to do, which was to take on interim executive roles or get myself elected onto various boards and committees like some sad old corporate brontosaurus who couldn't bear to give up their old life. I do not think others who do these things are dinosaurs, by the way. It is just how it would feel to me. Since the summer of 2014, when I finally hung up my chief executive boots, I've been helping others in various ways to be the best version of themselves. Coaching, speaking at events and via the media, and volunteering with charities that help others. I write most days and fit the other things around it. I've got more writing projects in my head than I will probably find space in this lifetime to finish. My novel is half written, and I'm itching to devote some solid time to it. I love the days when I start writing early in the morning and find myself, still in my pyjamas, late in the afternoon, having no idea where the day has gone. It takes discipline to write, but you have to love doing it. It is not for everyone. But for me, it is satisfying intellectually and emotionally.

I'm not saying you need to have your next career move all mapped out before you plan to leave. But do please allow yourself time to think about it before it happens to you.

In other words, try not to do what I did. Although, in the end it seems to be working out quite well.

Whose side are you on?

Some very nice things have happened since I retired in the summer of 2014. One of them was to be named as one of 50 Patient Leaders by the *Health Service Journal* the following summer.

And I was in amazing company. It was gratifying that I already knew quite a few of the people who were also on the list, such as Alison Cameron, David Gilbert, Ian Callaghan, James Titcombe and the parents of dear, departed but never to be forgotten young Adam Bojelian. It was lovely to meet many more at the event *HSJ* held for us in Leeds.

But this brings me a question, for myself and then for you. Can someone who has held a position of power and authority like mine ever truly be considered a patient leader? When the chips are down, who do I identify with most these days? Do I have I the right to stand alongside people who have experienced a considerably rougher ride than me?

It's a difficult question. It has taken events like the row over the junior doctors' dispute, the publication of the Mental Health Taskforce Report, and the struggles we have had with the Time to Change Mental Health Professionals project to make me realise that straddling a number of fences is extremely uncomfortable and neither satisfying nor effective. You have to come down on one side.

For me, the side I feel most comfortable on, ever since I started my NHS career in 1973 and met those dear little ones at the Forest Hospital, is with those people who are patients. It is they, or rather us, with whom I identify most. Because that is where I started when I met my first psychiatrist aged 15. And anyway, it is what we are all there for. It was at those times when I became confused about which side of the fence to place myself that I made my worst mistakes.

So to finish, I say this to any NHS leader or potential leader who is contemplating such a role. Even if you don't experience the double-edged benefits I have had from being both a patient and a leader simultaneously, I can promise you this. Life will be a lot simpler, albeit occasionally more challenging, if you remember that it is patients who always come first. Open your doors wide and welcome them in; they will help you make the most difficult decisions. They will even make some of them for you if you treat them with respect, do whatever it takes to enable them to build a trusting relationship with you, and listen really carefully to what they have to tell you.

If you have read my book and decided to give NHS leadership a go, I thank you with all my heart for choosing this most challenging but also vital role. Please let me know how you get on. I would really love to hear from you.

I close as I started, by wishing you luck, which you will need in bucket loads. But most of all, I wish you love.

Being an NHS Chief Executive

CONTACT ME

If you have enjoyed this book, you might like to visit me at my blog, *Lisa Says This*

www.LisaSaysThis.com/

You can find me on Twitter @LisaSaysThis

Being an NHS Chief Executive

Being an NHS Chief Executive

28283571R00140

Printed in Great Britain
by Amazon